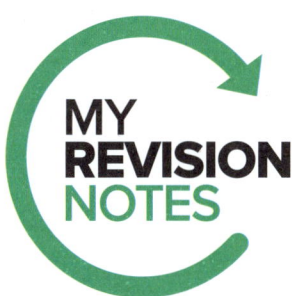 

CHILD DEVELOPMENT AND CARE IN THE EARLY YEARS

Louise Burnham

Penny Tassoni

Although every effort has been made to ensure that website addresses are correct at time of going to press, Hodder Education cannot be held responsible for the content of any website mentioned in this book. It is sometimes possible to find a relocated web page by typing in the address of the home page for a website in the URL window of your browser.

Hachette UK's policy is to use papers that are natural, renewable and recyclable products and made from wood grown in well-managed forests and other controlled sources. The logging and manufacturing processes are expected to conform to the environmental regulations of the country of origin.

Orders: please contact Hachette UK Distribution, Hely Hutchinson Centre, Milton Road, Didcot, Oxfordshire, OX11 7HH. Telephone: +44 (0)1235 827827. Email education@hachette.co.uk Lines are open from 9 a.m. to 5 p.m., Monday to Friday. You can also order through our website: www.hoddereducation.co.uk

ISBN: 9781398376281

© Penny Tassoni and Louise Burnham 2023

First published in 2023 by
Hodder Education,
An Hachette UK Company
Carmelite House
50 Victoria Embankment
London EC4Y 0DZ
www.hoddereducation.co.uk

Impression number   10 9 8 7 6 5 4 3 2 1

Year   2027 2026 2025 2024 2023

All rights reserved. Apart from any use permitted under UK copyright law, no part of this publication may be reproduced or transmitted in any form or by any means, electronic or mechanical, including photocopying and recording, or held within any information storage and retrieval system, without permission in writing from the publisher or under licence from the Copyright Licensing Agency Limited. Further details of such licences (for reprographic reproduction) may be obtained from the Copyright Licensing Agency Limited, www.cla.co.uk

Cover photo © Hiroki Obara - stock.adobe.com

Illustrations by Integra Software Services Pvt. Ltd., Pondicherry, India

Typeset by Integra Software Services Pvt. Ltd., Pondicherry, India

Printed in Spain

A catalogue record for this title is available from the British Library.

Get the most from this book

Everyone has to decide their own revision strategy, but it is essential to review your work, learn it and test your understanding. These Revision Notes will help you to do that in a planned way, topic by topic. Use this book as the cornerstone of your revision and don't hesitate to write in it — personalise your notes and check your progress by ticking off each section as you revise.

Tick to track your progress

Use the revision planner on pages 4 and 5 to plan your revision, topic by topic. Tick each box when you have:
+ revised and understood a topic
+ tested yourself
+ practised the exam questions and gone online to check your answers and complete the quick quizzes.

You can also keep track of your revision by ticking off each topic heading in the book. You may find it helpful to add your own notes as you work through each topic.

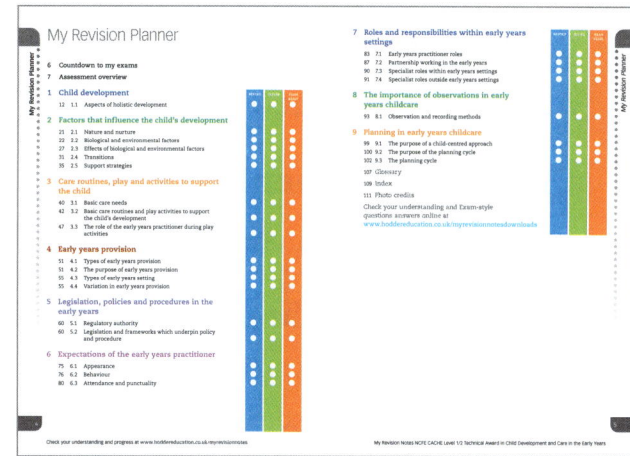

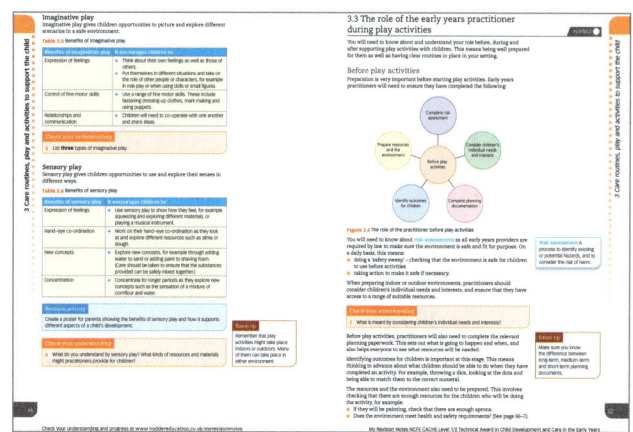

Features to help you succeed

Exam tips
Expert tips are given throughout the book to help you polish your exam technique in order to maximise your chances in the exam.

Typical mistakes
The authors identify the typical mistakes candidates make and explain how you can avoid them.

Check your understanding
These short, knowledge-based questions provide the first step in testing your learning. Answers are provided online.

Definitions and key words
Clear, concise definitions of essential key terms are provided where they first appear.

Key words from the specification are highlighted in blue throughout the book.

Revision activities
These activities will help you to understand each topic in an interactive way.

Use your knowledge
Questions at the end of each chapter to test your knowledge in real life situations.

Exam-style questions
Practice exam questions are provided for each topic. Use them to consolidate your revision and practise your exam skills. Answers are provided online.

Online
Go online to check your answers to the Check your understanding and Exam-style questions at **www.hoddereducation.co.uk/myrevisionnotesdownloads**

My Revision Notes NCFE CACHE Level 1/2 Technical Award in Child Development and Care in the Early Years

My Revision Planner

6 Countdown to my exams

7 Assessment overview

1 Child development
- 12   1.1   Aspects of holistic development

2 Factors that influence the child's development
- 21   2.1   Nature and nurture
- 22   2.2   Biological and environmental factors
- 27   2.3   Effects of biological and environmental factors
- 31   2.4   Transitions
- 35   2.5   Support strategies

3 Care routines, play and activities to support the child
- 40   3.1   Basic care needs
- 42   3.2   Basic care routines and play activities to support the child's development
- 47   3.3   The role of the early years practitioner during play activities

4 Early years provision
- 51   4.1   Types of early years provision
- 51   4.2   The purpose of early years provision
- 55   4.3   Types of early years setting
- 55   4.4   Variation in early years provision

5 Legislation, policies and procedures in the early years
- 60   5.1   Regulatory authority
- 60   5.2   Legislation and frameworks which underpin policy and procedure

6 Expectations of the early years practitioner
- 75   6.1   Appearance
- 76   6.2   Behaviour
- 80   6.3   Attendance and punctuality

Check your understanding and progress at www.hoddereducation.co.uk/myrevisionnotes

7 Roles and responsibilities within early years settings

- 83   7.1   Early years practitioner roles
- 87   7.2   Partnership working in the early years
- 90   7.3   Specialist roles within early years settings
- 91   7.4   Specialist roles outside early years settings

8 The importance of observations in early years childcare

- 93   8.1   Observation and recording methods

9 Planning in early years childcare

- 99   9.1   The purpose of a child-centred approach
- 100   9.2   The purpose of the planning cycle
- 102   9.3   The planning cycle

- 107   Glossary
- 109   Index
- 111   Photo credits

Check your understanding and Exam-style questions answers online at
www.hoddereducation.co.uk/myrevisionnotesdownloads

Countdown to my exams

From September

Attend class in person or online if necessary; listen and enjoy the subject; make notes. Make friends in class and discuss the topics with them. Watch the news.

REVISED ○

6–8 weeks to go

+ Start by looking at the specification – make sure you know exactly what material you need to revise and the style of the examination. Use the revision planner on pages 4 and 5 to familiarise yourself with the topics.
+ Organise your notes, making sure you have covered everything on the specification. The revision planner will help you to group your notes into topics.
+ Work out a realistic revision plan that will allow you time for relaxation. Set aside days and times for all the subjects that you need to study, and stick to your timetable.
+ Set yourself sensible targets. Break your revision down into focused sessions of around 40 minutes, divided by breaks. These Revision Notes organise the basic facts into short, memorable sections to make revising easier.

REVISED ○

2–6 weeks to go

+ Read through the relevant sections of this book and refer to the exam tips, typical mistakes and key terms. Tick off the topics as you feel confident about them. Highlight those topics you find difficult and look at them again in detail.
+ Test your understanding of each topic by working through the 'Check your understanding' questions in the book. Look up the answers online at **www.hoddereducation.co.uk/myrevisionnotesdownloads**.
+ Make a note of any problem areas as you revise and ask your teacher to go over these in class.
+ Look at past papers. They are one of the best ways to revise and practise your exam skills. Write or prepare planned answers to the exam-style questions provided in this book. Check your answers online at **www.hoddereducation.co.uk/myrevisionnotesdownloads**.
+ Use the revision activities to try out different revision methods. For example, you can make notes using mind maps, spider diagrams or flash cards.
+ Track your progress using the revision planner and give yourself a reward when you have achieved your target.

REVISED ○

One week to go

+ Try to fit in at least one more timed practice of an entire past paper and seek feedback from your teacher, comparing your work closely with the mark scheme.
+ Check the revision planner to make sure you haven't missed out any topics. Brush up on any areas of difficulty by talking them over with a friend or getting help from your teacher.
+ Attend any revision classes put on by your teacher. Remember, your teacher is an expert at preparing people for examinations.

REVISED ○

The day before the examination

+ Flick through these Revision Notes for useful reminders, for example, the exam tips, typical mistakes and key terms.
+ IMPORTANT: Check the time (is it morning or afternoon?) and place of your examination. Keep in touch with other students in your class.
+ Make sure you have everything you need for the exam – pens, highlighters and water.
+ Allow some time to relax and have an early night to ensure you are fresh and alert.

REVISED ○

My exams

Paper A

Date:..

Time: ....

Location: ....

Paper B

Date:..

Time: ....

Location: ....

Check your understanding and progress at www.hoddereducation.co.uk/myrevisionnotes

Assessment overview

(The guidance below has not been reviewed by NCFE. You are strongly advised to refer to the NCFE website for the most up-to-date information on assessment, including sample exam papers, mark schemes and the latest specification.)

About this qualification

REVISED

Assessment for this qualification will be 50 per cent through a written examination and 50 per cent through a non-exam assessment (NEA).

You will have more time to do the NEA, which will assess how you apply your knowledge to real-life scenarios.

The marks that you get from the exam papers and the NEA are added together. Your overall marks will decide whether you get a Level 1 or Level 2 qualification. Both the written examination and the non-exam assessment will be designed with the following Assessment Objectives, or AOs:

+ AO1 Recall knowledge and show understanding
+ AO2 Apply knowledge and understanding
+ AO3 Analyse and evaluate knowledge and understanding

These are three types of skill you need to show as you answer different types of question in the exam and the various tasks in the NEA. These objectives describe what the questions are testing, and what your answer needs to show you can do. You will find these AOs next to the online answers to questions in this book.

For the NEA, you will also be assessed on the following AOs:

+ AO4 Demonstrate the application of relevant vocational skills, processes, working practices and documentation
+ AO5 Analyse and evaluate the demonstration of relevant vocational skills, processes, working practices and documentation

The Use your knowledge features at the end of each chapter will help you prepare for this as you will be showing that you can apply your knowledge and skills in real life situations.

Preparing for the Non-Exam Assessment (NEA)

The NEA is made up of several tasks, and assesses your knowledge and understanding across all the units of the qualification. The tasks are based on a real-life scenario. You will complete the tasks over several sessions in exam conditions.
+ You will have a total of 14 hours to complete the tasks.
+ You can decide how much time to spend on each task.
+ At the end of each session, you cannot take your work away.
+ You cannot ask for information or advice from your tutor or classmates.

Before the first NEA session, find out from your tutor what resources, if any, you can take in and whether there will be any resources available in the supervised sessions. Use this information to help you plan your revision.

There are many different ways in which you could be asked to present information, such as a:
+ report
+ leaflet
+ letter
+ detailed plan
+ risk assessment form
+ chart.

Make sure that you have practised presenting information in these different formats.

During the NEA sessions
When the NEA is given to you:
1 Listen carefully to what you are allowed and not allowed to do during the session.
2 Read through the case study carefully, and each of the tasks.
3 Choose one task to focus on.
4 Go back and reread the case study. Underline or take notes about anything that you think will be important.
5 Read carefully how your answer needs to be presented.
6 Keep an eye on the time.
7 If you get stuck, start looking at another task.
8 If you are using paper to write on, make sure that you leave space between the lines so that you can cross things out and add new information if you need. After each session, write down what you have completed and what you need to do next, so that you can remember it more quickly next time.

Use the time you have between sessions to help you plan for your next session.

Do not panic if a session has not gone well. Instead, think about what you need to know and do when it is time for the next session.

At the start of each new session:
+ Reread the case study and the task that you are working on.
+ Read through what you have written, but do not start again. If you have time after completing each of the tasks, you can make changes then.

In the final session:
+ If you have finished all the tasks, spend your time rereading your work. If you have time, you can add to your work. On handwritten tasks, you can start a new piece of paper if you do not have space under your first answer.
+ If you start a new piece of paper, make sure that you write the number of the task that it is for and put an asterisk (*) on your first answer to show that you want to add something.

Peter is four years old. His physical development is not typical for his age. * I would advise that he is given more access to the outdoor area where he can learn new physical skills.	Task 3 * He has just started to run and this is not typical of most four-year-olds' gross motor skills. It might be that he has not had enough space to move around at home as he lives in a small flat and a built-up area.

Preparing for the exams
Before each exam you need to go over your work carefully to make sure that you have learned the materials.

On the day of the exam
Make sure you take into the exam only what you need. You should have a blue or black pen. You will be able to do any rough work or working out on the exam paper and you can cross through any mistakes.

The exam will be 1.5 hours long and will have 4 sections: A, B, C and D. The front of the exam paper will tell you how long to spend on each section and how many marks you will be awarded for each correct answer. There are 80 marks available in total for the whole paper.

Remember to read through the whole paper and try to answer all the questions. Read through each question twice before answering to make sure you understand what is being asked. Try not to worry if there are some that you are not able to answer; concentrate on doing the ones that you can first.

Check your understanding and progress at www.hoddereducation.co.uk/myrevisionnotes

Question types

You will find three types of questions in the exam paper:
+ multiple-choice questions
+ short-answer questions
+ extended response questions.

It will help you to know about each type of question so that you know what to expect.

Multiple-choice questions

Some questions in the exam will be multiple choice. To answer these, you need to choose the right answer from a choice of four. Here is an example:

1 Which one of these is a notifiable disease?
   A chickenpox
   B mumps
   C impetigo
   D flu   [1]

In order to tackle this question, think about what is meant by a notifiable disease to help you to identify which is the correct answer. (The correct answer to this question is B.)

Tips for multiple-choice questions:
+ Always read through all answers before making a decision.
+ Sometimes more than one answer will seem possible, but one will always be the right one in that situation.
+ If you do not know the answer, have a guess.

Short-answer questions

Short-answer questions usually ask you to write one or two sentences. Sometimes you may be asked to complete a chart or a table.

Look to see how many marks the question is worth. Two marks might mean that you need to put down two pieces of information.

These kinds of questions are made up of command words such as 'identify', 'explain' or 'describe'. Command words tell you what you need to do to answer the question. Look carefully at these before writing the answer, as the correct type of answer and how detailed it is will depend on the command.

Look at this table, which explains the meaning of different command words. These verbs are most likely to be used in short-answer questions.

Command words in short-answer questions

Command word	Use
Compare	Look at similarities and differences.
Describe	Write about the main characteristics.
Explain	Make something clear by setting out the main purpose or reason, giving evidence.
Identify	Name, choose or recognise.
Outline	Set out the main points or features.
State	Write about in clear terms.
Summarise	Briefly present the main points.

> **Revision activity**
>
> Match each command word to its correct definition:
>
> | | |
> |---|---|
> | Identify | Make something clear by setting out the main purpose or reason, giving evidence. |
> | Explain | Write about the main characteristics. |
> | Describe | Name, choose or recognise. |

> **Typical mistake**
>
> Remember not to write more information than is needed in a short-answer question. If you do, you will not have enough time to complete the extended response questions.

Here is an example of a short-answer question:

2 Give **two** reasons why confidentiality must be maintained in early years settings. [2]

To tackle this question:
+ First think about what confidentiality means.
+ Decide which two reasons you are going to give. You do not need to give more.
+ For example: 'Confidentiality must be maintained in early years settings because it is a legal requirement and because it builds trust between those who care for the child.'
+ Keep to the point when answering. You will not gain more marks because you have written a longer answer.

Extended response questions

There will also be a small number of questions that require a longer answer, and more marks will be available for these questions.

Extended response questions usually require you to show that you are able to analyse information and also apply knowledge to a given situation. You may include an example to make your point.

Command words in extended response questions

Command words	Use
Analyse	Look at different parts and examine them in detail to show meaning.
Assess	Think about and evaluate.
Consider	Review/respond to information which has been given.
Describe	Write about the main characteristics.
Discuss	Write about key points of different ideas, presenting strengths and weaknesses.
Evaluate	Review and judge the information given to draw conclusions.
Explain	Make something clear by setting out the main purpose or reason, giving evidence.
Justify	Support a case with evidence.
Show	Give evidence which leads to a conclusion.
Suggest	Apply knowledge to a new situation and present a possible solution.
Summarise	Briefly present the main points.
Use or using	The answer should refer to and be based on information which has been given in the question.

Note: the command words 'describe' and 'explain' may be used in both short-answer and extended response questions.

Figure 1.1 Which areas of development are these children using?

> **Exam tip**
>
> Make sure that you understand why each area of development is important for children.
>
> It might help you to imagine a child being able to doing something specific, such as playing with a ball with a sibling.

> **Check your understanding**
>
> 1 Write down the **four** different areas of development.

> **Revision activity**
>
> Make a set of four flashcards.
> + On one side, write the name of an area of development.
> + On the other side, write what it involves.
>
> Test yourself by looking at a card and remembering what is on the other side.

Holistic development

Development is split into four areas, but they are all connected to one another. The term holistic development is about how the different aspects of development link together.

> **Holistic development**
> How different aspects of development are linked together.

> **Revision activity**
>
> Here are two examples of how different areas of development link together.
> + A three-year-old child **asks** another child to play **with her** – the area of communication and language is linked to social and emotional development.
> + A four-year-old child **works out** that he needs to **turn** a shape round to fit in a puzzle – cognitive and physical development are linked together here.
>
> Now look at this example and say how three different areas of development link together:
> + A three-year-old child **pours** a drink from a jug. She **says**, 'Look! I did that **all by myself**.'

Development follows a sequence

Adults working with children track development in each of the four areas because development follows a sequence or order.

If a child has not gained a skill, this will affect:
+ their progress in that area: a baby cannot walk until he has the skill of standing.
+ their overall area: when a baby learns to stand and then walk, she can see new things and explore more.

My Revision Notes NCFE CACHE Level 1/2 Technical Award in Child Development and Care in the Early Years

Adults working with children can look up the order and also the age by which children gain skills in each area of development. These skills are known as milestones. You need to learn the milestones for each area of development.

1.1.1 Physical development

Physical development is important. It helps children do things independently such as dress, reach for toys and feed themselves. It is also helps children to learn through play as they can touch things and explore.

Physical development is divided into large movements and small movements.
+ Small movements are called fine motor skills. Examples include holding a crayon and fastening a zip.
+ Large movements are called gross motor skills. Examples include walking, balancing and throwing.

> **Milestones** Skills that are expected at different ages.
>
> **Fine motor skills** Co-ordination of small muscles, precise movements and hand–eye co-ordination.
>
> **Gross motor skills** Co-ordination of the large muscles of the arms, legs and torso.

Revision activity

Look at these skills:
+ Points using index finger
+ Sits down from standing
+ Separates interlocking bricks
+ Runs with control (without bumping into things)
+ Can kick, throw and bounce a ball
+ Draws lines, dots and circles
+ Begins to fasten buttons
+ Can walk backwards.

Decide whether they are examples of fine motor or gross motor skills. Copy out this table and write the skills in the correct column. The first two have been done for you.

Fine motor skills	Gross motor skills
Points using index finger	Sits down from standing

> **Typical mistake**
>
> Make sure you don't write about a gross motor skill when the question is about fine motor skills.

Key milestones in physical development

You will need to learn the key milestones for fine and gross motor skills in Tables 1.2 and 1.3 for each age group. Allow plenty of time to revise these milestones. You are likely to be asked a question about them or need the information to answer a case study.

Table 1.2 Key milestones for fine motor skills

Age of child	Fine motor skill milestones – the child will typically:
At birth	+ have their hands firmly closed + often fold their thumb under their fingers
1 year	+ point using their index finger + pass and release toys + clasp their hands together + hold a crayon with palmar grasp and make random marks
2 years	+ be able to pull apart interlocking toys + use a pincer grip to pick up small objects + be able to draw lines, dots and circles
3 years	+ begin to show a preference for their dominant hand (left or right) + be able to fasten a large zip + be able to draw a person with a head
4 years	+ begin to fasten buttons + be able to use a spoon and fork well to eat + be able to draw a figure that resembles a person showing head, legs and body
5 years	+ be able to use a knife and fork competently + be able to thread small beads + be able to draw a person with a head, body, arms, legs, nose and mouth

> **Palmar grasp** Object is held in the child's fist
>
> **Pincer grip** Object is held between thumb and forefinger or middle finger

Check your understanding and progress at www.hoddereducation.co.uk/myrevisionnotes

> **Check your understanding**
>
> 2 At what age will a child be able to thread small beads?

> **Revision activity**
>
> Write down each of the milestones on separate pieces of paper. Shuffle them up.
> + Group the milestones into ages.
> + Ask someone to pick a milestone out and read it to you. Can you identify the age being described?

You need to learn the key milestones for gross motor skills.

Table 1.3 Milestones for gross motor skills

Age of child	Gross motor skill milestones – a child will typically:
At birth	+ lie on their back with head to one side + lag their head when pulled to sitting position
1 year	+ stand and may **cruise** around furniture + sit down from standing + become more mobile
2 years	+ walk up and down stairs by holding adult's hand + run with control + throw and kick a ball
3 years	+ walk backwards and sideways + ride and steer a tricycle + jump from a low step with both feet together + throw a ball overhand and can catch a large ball with arms outstretched
4 years	+ stand and run on tiptoe + hop + change direction while running + catch, kick, throw and bounce a ball
5 years	+ skip and move rhythmically to music + hop on each foot + ride bicycle with stabilisers

> **Cruise** How babies walk about by holding onto furniture.

> **Revision activity**
>
> Write down each of the gross motor skill milestones on separate pieces of paper. Shuffle them up.
> + Group the milestones into ages.
> + Repeat this, but now add the fine motor skill milestones.

> **Check your understanding**
>
> 3 What is meant by the term 'milestone'?

> **Revision activity**
>
> Copy out this table:
>
> | Age | Fine motor skill milestones | Gross motor skill milestones |
> |---|---|---|
> | At birth | Have their hands firmly closed | |
> | 1 year | | |
> | 2 years | Use pincer grip to pick up small objects | |
> | 3 years | | |
> | 4 years | | |
> | 5 years | | Skips and moves rhythmically to music |
>
> From memory, write down as many fine and gross motor milestones as you can for each age.
>
> Check Tables 1.2 and 1.3 to see which skills you missed.

1.1.2 Cognitive development

Cognitive development helps us to remember things, organise our ideas and solve problems. It develops over time.

You need to learn the key milestones for cognitive development. Allow plenty of time for this. You may find it easier to learn the milestones for babies separately.

Babies: cognitive development and reflexes

Reflexes such as crying and rooting help babies to survive. These are known as primitive reflexes. Over time many will disappear as babies learn how to make movements by themselves.

Table 1.4 Cognitive development milestones for babies

Age of child	Cognitive development milestones
At birth	A baby will typically: + turn their head towards bright light + like looking at high-contrast patterns, e.g. black and white shapes + be startled by sudden noises + show a range of primitive reflexes, such as swallow and suck, show the rooting (looking for milk) reflex, grasp and step + show the asymmetric tonic neck reflex and Moro reflex (a movement when startled).

> **Primitive reflexes** Movements that newborns make automatically.
>
> **Rooting** A reflex in newborn babies to search for milk using their mouth.
>
> **Asymmetric tonic neck reflex (ATNR)** A reflex where if the baby's head is turned to one side, the knee and arm on the other side bend.
>
> **Moro reflex** A reflex where the baby throws back head and arms, then brings them in before crying.

Revision activity

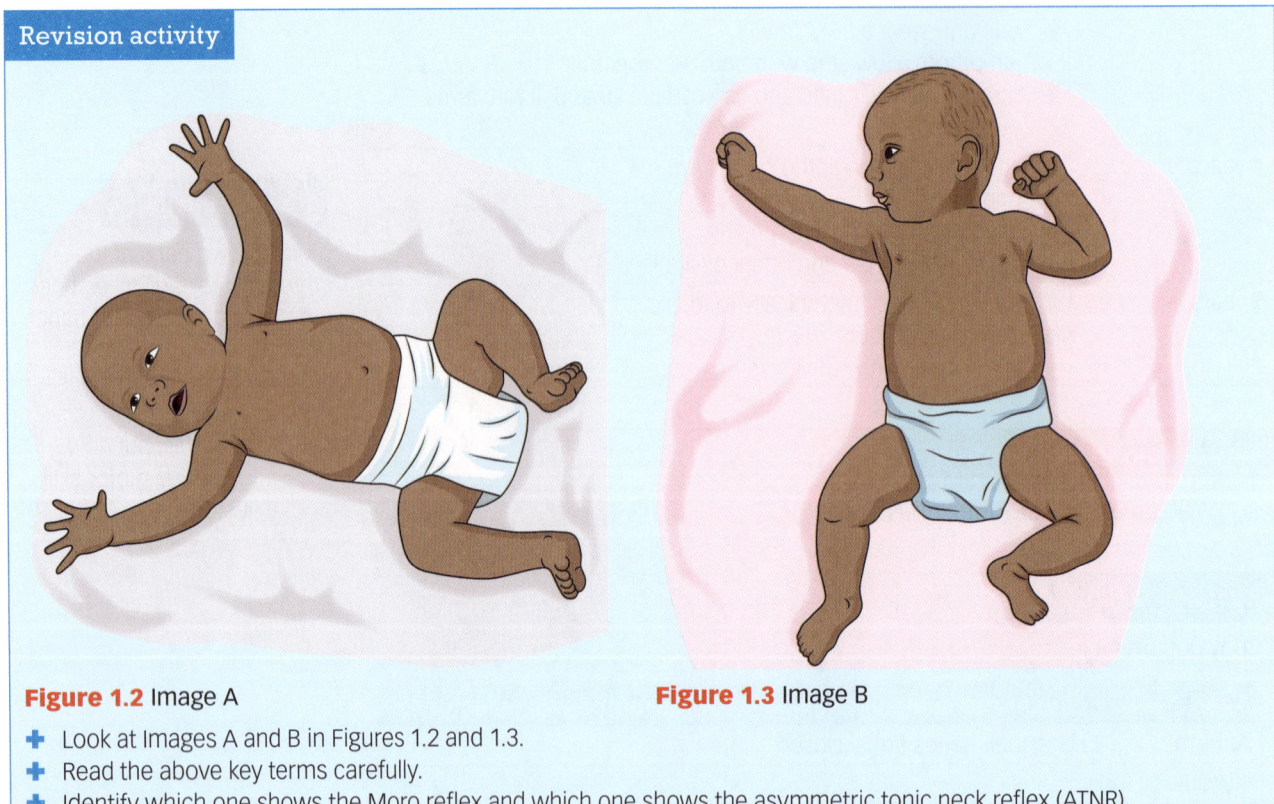

Figure 1.2 Image A

Figure 1.3 Image B

+ Look at Images A and B in Figures 1.2 and 1.3.
+ Read the above key terms carefully.
+ Identify which one shows the Moro reflex and which one shows the asymmetric tonic neck reflex (ATNR).

Cognitive skills

Table 1.5 Cognitive development milestones for children from one to five years

Age of child	At the end of this stage, a child will typically:
1 year	+ understand simple instructions such as 'clap hands' + imitate and respond to gestures + anticipate future routines

Table 1.5 Continued

Age of child	At the end of this stage, a child will typically:
2 years	+ understand that a mirror is a reflection + begin to understand the consequences of their own actions + name pictures and objects in a book
3 years	+ recognise objects that are heavy and light + show awareness of past and present + actively seek answers to questions – using 'Why?' + sort objects by size and shape
4 years	+ name some colours + count to 10 + recall stories and rhymes + become confused between fantasy and reality
5 years	+ give meaning to marks they make and see + count up to 20 + understand basic rules + become interested in reading and writing

Revision activity

Look at the table, which shows how many cognitive development milestones there are to remember for each age group. Complete the table.

Age	Number of milestones
At birth	5
1 year	
2 years	
3 years	
4 years	
5 years	4

Choose an age group and see how many milestones you can remember. Go back to Tables 1.4 and 1.5, which show the different milestones and check how you did.

1.1.3 Communication and language development

Communication and language is about the ability to understand others, but also to communicate with others. It is important in helping children express their needs and feelings. It also helps them to understand others and follow instructions.

You will need to learn the milestones for communication and language shown in Table 1.6.

Table 1.6 Milestones for communication and language

Age	Communication and language milestones – a child will typically:
At birth	+ recognise mother's or main carer's voice + not be able to hear very soft sounds + cry to indicate need
1 year	+ babble tunefully, leading to first single spoken words + raise tone to gain attention + follow simple instructions and understand simple frequent words
2 years	+ use 50 words or more + join two words together + refer to self by name + understand a wide range of words

Table 1.6 Continued

Age	Communication and language milestones – a child will typically:
3 years	+ use 200 words or more + ask questions constantly, using what, why, who + join in simple rhymes
4 years	+ be understood easily by others + enjoy telling and sharing stories + know several nursery rhymes and songs
5 years	+ begin to show signs of reading + concentrate and maintain attention + use language and gestures to convey meaning + use speech which is mostly grammatically correct

> **Revision activity**
>
> Development follows a sequence. Create a timeline that shows how children learn to understand and talk:
> + Using six pieces of paper (one for each age group), write the milestones for talking on one side.
> + On the other side, write the milestones about listening and understanding.
>
> Mix up the pieces of paper and then put them in age group order.

1.1.4 Social and emotional development

Social and emotional development are often put together as they are closely linked:
+ Social development is about learning to be with others and knowing how to behave in different situations.
+ Emotional development is about managing feelings and impulses. It is also about confidence.

You will need to learn the milestones for social and emotional development for different ages of children.

Table 1.7 Social and emotional development milestones

Age	Social and emotional milestones – a child will typically:
At birth	+ imitate facial expressions + express pleasure at bath time or when being fed + enjoy physical touch
1 year	+ enjoy playing simple games such as 'peek a boo' + cry if unable to see their carer + be dependent on others + play alone or alongside others happily
2 years	+ be confident and curious to explore the environment + feel frustrated when unable to express feelings + be clingy at times but independent at others
3 years	+ enjoy playing with other children + express emotions + enjoy imaginative and creative play experiences + like to do tasks unaided
4 years	+ welcome and value praise + be more confident in new situations and with unfamiliar adults + be sensitive to others + become fearful as imagination increases
5 years	+ enjoy group play + have definite likes and dislikes + describe self in a positive way + gain confidence, become more independent

> **Revision activity**
>
> Using the milestones in Table 1.7, make a timeline with steps that show how children become more confident and independent.

Check your understanding and progress at www.hoddereducation.co.uk/myrevisionnotes

Figure 1.4 Having friends is linked to social and emotional development

> **Revision activity**
>
> Find six pieces of paper or card. Each piece of paper or card will be for a specific age group of children.
> - Choose an age group and write it on the back of one of the pieces of paper or card.
> - Now fold it in half.
> - On one side of the folded paper or card, write down the milestones for communication and language.
> - On the other side, write down the milestones for social and emotional development.
> - Repeat this for the other age groups.
>
> Test yourself to see if you can identify the age group by reading the milestones on one side of the card.

> **Typical mistake**
>
> Don't forget that social and emotional development is linked to communication and language. Children need social and emotional skills in order to communicate and understand others.

> **Revision activity**
>
> Look at this table. Which age group is it for? Check back with the milestones tables.

Communication and language	Cognitive
+ uses 50 words or more + joins two words together + refers to self by name + understands a wide range of words	+ understands that a mirror is a reflection + begins to understand the consequences of their own actions + names pictures and objects in a book
Physical	**Social and emotional**
+ is able to pull apart interlocking toys + uses pincer grip to pick up small objects + can draw lines, dots and circles + walks up and down stairs by holding adult's hand + runs with control + throws and kicks a ball	+ is confident and curious to explore the environment + often feels frustrated when unable to express feelings + may be clingy at times but independent at others

Make tables like this for each of the other age groups.

> **Exam tip**
>
> Make sure that you know the milestones for each age group across the four areas of development. This will help you answer a case study question about a child's development.

> **Revision activity**
>
> Write down as many milestones as you can remember in each area for a three-year-old child.
>
> Go back to the milestones tables to see which ones you had forgotten.

Exam-style questions

1. Managing feelings is an example of which area of development?
   - A Cognitive development
   - B Communication and language development
   - C Social and emotional development
   - D Physical development [1]

2. Explain with examples how each of the areas of development support a four-year-old's ability to play with others. [8]

3. Explain with examples how **three** of the areas of development support a four-year-old's ability to play with others. [6]

4. Explain, with an example, how cognitive development is linked to physical development. [2]

5. Which of these tasks can most three-year-olds do?
   - A Use a knife and fork competently
   - B Thread small beads
   - C Cut out a star shape
   - D Fasten a large zip [1]

6. a) Define the term 'gross motor skill'. [1]
   b) Give an example of an action showing gross motor movement for a two-year-old. [1]

7. State **two** gross motor milestones for a three-year-old. [2]

8. By what age can children order objects by size?
   - A One year
   - B Two years
   - C Three years
   - D Four years [1]

9. State **one** example of a reflex that a newborn baby will show. [1]

10. Which **one** of the following can a two-year-old typically do?
    - A Babble tunefully
    - B Ask simple questions
    - C Use 50 words
    - D Show signs of reading [1]

11. Which **one** of the following is an example of a social and emotional milestone of a child aged three years?
    - A Enjoys playing with other children
    - B Cries if unable to see their carer
    - C Sorts objects by shape and size
    - D Runs on tiptoe [1]

12. A one-year-old in a nursery is starting to walk. Discuss how this may affect the child's holistic development. [6]

Use your knowledge

Aran is four years old. He is about to start a nursery class. His parents have filled in this form about his development at home:

What does Aran like doing?	What does Aran find difficult?
Aran likes riding his bicycle. Aran likes puzzles and loves using pens and markers to draw with. He loves cuddling up with us on the sofa.	Aran finds it hard to play with other children. He often snatches things or hits out at them.
What can Aran do by himself?	**What would you like Aran to do next?**
He can dress himself although he cannot do laces yet. He is toilet-trained. He can use a spoon and fork and sometimes a knife.	He doesn't talk as much as other children. He tends to point at things. It would be good if he could have more confidence. He is often clingy and does not like trying out new things.

The nursery manager also spoke to Aran's parents to find out more about his communication and language development. This is what they said to her:

'Aran tends to point at things as he only has a few words. He does say mummy and daddy, and he also has a word for the cat. He becomes upset when we can't understand what he wants. He can follow simple instructions.'

The nursery has asked you to write a short report about Aran's holistic development in each of the four areas of development.

+ Your report should identify areas of development which are typical as well as those that are not.
+ Your report should also refer to the key milestones for each of the areas of development.

Check your understanding and progress at www.hoddereducation.co.uk/myrevisionnotes

2 Factors that influence the child's development

This chapter looks at why children might show differences in their development. It also discusses what happens when changes takes place in children's lives. These changes are called transitions.

> **Exam tip**
>
> Revise this chapter by splitting the content in two:
> 1. Factors affecting development (sections 2.1–2.3)
> 2. Transitions (sections 2.4–2.5).
>
> Make sure that you spend roughly equal time on both sections. It is likely that there will be questions on both.

2.1 Nature and nurture

REVISED

When we look at children of the same age, we will find many differences between them. The nature/nurture debate is about why these different characteristics and other differences between individuals exist.
+ The nature side of the debate suggests that many of the differences are decided before we are born. These are often called biological influences.
+ The nurture side of the debate suggests that the differences result from what has happened to children since they were born. These are called environmental influences.

> **Biological influences** Things that are a result of the way that we have been made.
>
> **Environmental influences** Things that have happened and are happening to a child that will affect their development.

> **Revision activity**
>
> Look at these statements. Decide whether they are true or false.
> + An example of a characteristic due to nature is the colour of your eyes.
> + An example of a characteristic due to nature is being able to read.
> + An example of a characteristic due to nurture is knowing how to use a computer.
>
> (Hint: if the characteristics are things that can be taught or copied, they link to nurture.)

Nature – biological influences

Nature is about our individual biology: the way our body and our brain have come together, and our development. So our biological influences are things affected by the ways our bodies are created.

Genetic

Cells are the building blocks for our bodies. Chromosomes are structures that are found inside of cells. Cells contain 23 pairs of chromosomes. Each chromosome has its own genes. Genes contains sets of instructions that affect whether and how cells grow and develop.

In some cases, genes can have missing or extra parts. This can cause a range of health problems and learning disabilities, which we say are genetic.

> **Genes** Chromosomes that contain instructions about whether and how cells grow.
>
> **Genetic** Relating to genes.

Inherited characteristics

Many aspects of a child's health and development can be traced back to their biological family. If a family member has ginger hair, a baby may be born with ginger hair.

In some cases, medical conditions and learning disabilities can run in families. When something can be genetically traced back to the biological family, we say it is an inherited characteristic.

Inherited characteristics Things that can be traced back to a child's biological family.

Eczema A skin condition that causes dry and itchy skin.

Nurture – environmental influences

Nurture is about environmental influences. These are things that a child has experienced since birth. They include whether the child's basic needs have been met, as well as what the child has done and been taught, and where they grow up.

The debate: how much nature and nurture impact child development

Researchers now believe that both nature and nurture come together to influence the health and development of a child. For example:
+ A child may be born with the gene responsible for eczema, but it only flares up when the child is feeling stressed.
+ The adults now know that if the child has eczema, they need to find ways of helping the child feel less stressed.

Exam tip

In questions about nature and nurture that start with 'evaluate' or 'discuss', your answer should show that you understand how they work together.

2.2 Biological and environmental factors

In this section, you will need to learn examples of biological and environmental factors that affect children's healthy growth and development.

Biological factors

This is linked to the nature part of development explored above.

Inherited or health conditions

Inherited biological factors can affect what children look like. This includes skin colour and height.

Some health conditions can also be linked to the biological family. An example of this is eczema. Eczema can be uncomfortable and it can prevent children from sleeping at night. This in turn can affect children's concentration and learning.

Exam tip

Make sure that you have learnt your environmental factors carefully. It is likely that you will need to write about one or more of them to answer a case study question.

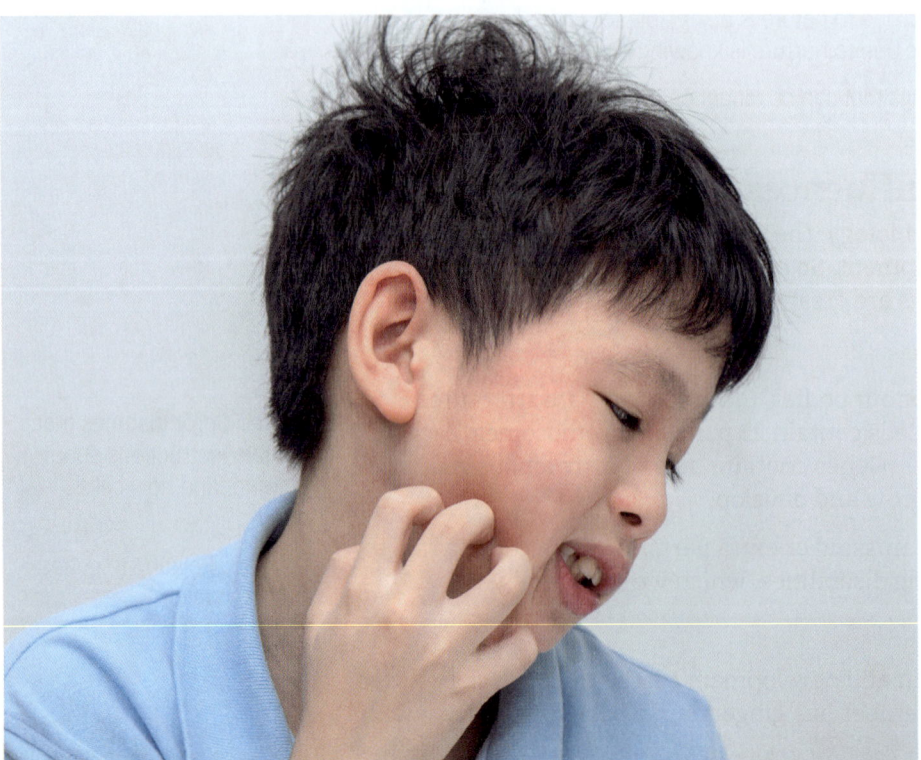

Figure 2.1 Eczema can affect all aspects of a child's development

Check your understanding and progress at www.hoddereducation.co.uk/myrevisionnotes

Muscle structure

Sometimes a copy of a faulty gene can pass on from the biological family to the child. This can cause health conditions that affect the muscles in the body.

An example of this is Duchenne muscular dystrophy. This is a serious health condition that causes the muscles to become weak. It has many effects on the development of children living with the condition; for example, they might not be able to join in physical games with other children. This can affect their emotional and social development.

Hair and eye colour

+ The colour and texture of hair is inherited from a child's biological family.
+ The colour of a child's eyes is also inherited.

Environmental factors

Immediate surroundings

The specification gives many examples of environmental factors in their immediate surroundings that affect a child's development. They include the child's experience of:
+ people
+ places
+ situations
+ circumstances
+ relationships.

Table 2.1 explains these points in more detail.

> **Exam tip**
>
> Remember that an environmental factor is anything that happens to children or that they experience **after** they are born.

Table 2.1 Environmental factors affecting development

Environmental factor	Explanation	Example
People	The people that children meet and also live with can affect development.	A child goes to pre-school and learns to play with other children.
Places	Where children live and where they go can affect development.	A child lives in a cramped flat and has no outdoor space. They do not have opportunities to play, and this affects their learning and therefore their cognitive development.
Situations	Things that happen to the child or the family.	A child falls down the stairs and breaks a leg. The child cannot run.
Circumstances	Conditions that affect what the child experiences.	A family are on a low income and cannot afford new shoes. The child does not like running because their shoes are too tight.
Relationships	Relationships with family members, neighbours and significant people affect development.	A child has a good relationship with their teacher. The child tries extra hard at school and makes good progress.

> **Revision activity**
>
> Copy out this table. For each environmental factor, think of an example and what it might mean for a child. The first has been done for you.
>
> | Environmental factor | The effect of this factor on a child's development |
> |---|---|
> | People | A child watches a painter. Afterwards the child is interested in painting. |
> | Places | |
> | Situations | |
> | Circumstances | |
> | Relationships | |

As well as revising the broad categories, you need also to learn some specific examples. Try to use your knowledge of the areas of development to think about how the factors may affect a child.

Inner city

Children living in city centres or urban areas may have more opportunities to do activities such as swimming or ice skating. They may also be able to go to cinemas and museums more easily.

Children living in the city may live in flats. They may miss out on playing outdoors because of a lack of outdoor space.

Rural areas

Children in *rural* areas might have opportunities to learn about nature (plants and animals) and spend time outdoors. They might not have as many opportunities to go to different places such as the cinema or to join cultural activities in urban areas.

Rural In the countryside.

> **Revision activity**
>
> Look at this list of opportunities:
> - able to play outdoors
> - able to visit museums and go to concerts
> - explore nature and the countryside
> - plenty of activities nearby.
>
> Decide which are more likely if a child lives in a rural area and which are more likely if a child lives in the inner city. Copy this table, and put each opportunity into the correct column.
>
> | Rural area | Inner city |
> |---|---|
> | | |

> **Check your understanding**
>
> 1. What does the term 'rural' mean?
> 2. Hunter lives with his family in a small village. The family do not have a car and so they walk everywhere. All the families in the village know each other well. The children play with each other in the countryside.
>   Explain how Hunter may benefit from growing up in a village.

Socio-economic factors

Socio-economic factors are about parents' or carers' income, social status and level of education. Parents in a high socio-economic group may have more choices about where they live and what they can provide for their child, such as clothes, toys and education.

When families live on a very low income, parents find it harder to afford things such as clothes, holidays and activities. They may not have much money for books and toys. The term *poverty* is used when the amount of money which a family has to live on is very low.

Poverty Living on a very low income and/or not having what you need.

Check your understanding and progress at **www.hoddereducation.co.uk/myrevisionnotes**

> **Check your understanding**
>
> 3 What does the term 'socio-economic factor' mean?

A child's home can affect their development:
+ When a family can afford good housing, children might have more space to play. They might also be able to have a pet.
+ When a family is living in a poor standard of housing, children might not have much space to play or be able to invite friends to visit them. It might also affect children's wellbeing if the housing is not safe or if it is damp, because they are more likely to get ill. Many families who rent homes are not allowed to keep a pet.

> **Check your understanding**
>
> 4 Look at the opportunities that some children have because of their families' socio-economic status. Link each opportunity to the area of development.
>
> | a | Space to play outdoors | 1 | Cognitive development: opportunities to experience new things |
> |---|---|---|---|
> | b | Go on holiday | 2 | Social and emotional development: being responsible and learning to care |
> | c | Have a pet | 3 | Language development: opportunities to talk while sharing books and playing games |
> | d | Have lots of books and games | 4 | Physical development: opportunities to move and develop skills |

Family lifestyle

The way that families live can make a difference to whether or not their children's needs are met. Note that a family might not be able to choose their lifestyle. Research shows a link between lifestyle and poverty. Table 2.2 shows how five aspects may affect children's development.

Table 2.2 The effect of lifestyle factors on children's development

Lifestyle factor	The effect on children's development
Abuse	+ There are different types of abuse: physical abuse, sexual abuse and emotional abuse, and also neglect (see Chapter 5). + Abuse affects children's social and emotional development as they might feel unloved or find it hard to trust people. + Some types of abuse can affect children's physical development such as fractures from physical abuse.
Neglect	+ Neglect is when children are not looked after properly. + Neglect occurs when parents or carers do not keep their children clean, feed them or keep them safe. + Children might have more health problems or accidents.
Drugs/alcohol	+ If parents or carers are using drugs and/or alcohol, they might not be meeting their children's basic needs including safety, food and cleanliness. + Parents using drugs and/or alcohol might not give their children consistent love and affection. + This affects children's social and emotional development.
Healthy diet	+ A healthy diet meets children's nutritional needs. + It will include fresh foods, vegetables, sources of protein such as fish and also carbohydrates such as rice and potato. + A healthy diet helps children to fight infection. + A healthy diet is important for growth and energy.
Poor diet	+ A poor diet might be high in fat and sugar but low in fresh foods. + A poor diet might give children more calories than they need. + It might cause tooth decay. + It might not help children fight infection + A poor diet might cause a child to be overweight and so physical activity may be harder.

> **Revision activity**
>
> **True or false?**
> Read the statements and decide which ones are true and which ones are false.
> + A poor diet is high in fresh foods.
> + A healthy diet can help fight infection.
> + Drug abuse can affect children's safety.
> + Abuse can help a child's social and emotional development.

> **Check your understanding**
>
> 5 Imran is four years old. His family eats a lot of unhealthy snacks and junk food. He often does not have a healthy breakfast but snacks on biscuits and crisps instead.
>
> What are the possible effects of Imran's diet on his health and development?

Opportunities for exercise

Some children have more opportunities for exercise than others. Exercise is important for health and also physical development.

> **Check your understanding**
>
> 6 Andre and his family live in a small flat in the inner city. They have no garden and not much space indoors. The family struggle to have enough money. There is a swimming pool and sports club nearby, but his family cannot afford to go there.
>
> Give **two** environmental factors that might affect Andre's physical development.

Stimulation

Children who have stimulation make progress with their overall development. You need to remember at least two ways to stimulate children. Table 2.3 shows two ways and gives examples.

Table 2.3 Stimulation for children

Type of stimulation	Examples
A language-rich environment	Children in this environment have opportunities to: + chat to responsive adults and also other children + share books + listen to stories and talk.
Play experiences	Children who have a variety of play experiences have opportunities to: + play indoors with a range of toys and resources + explore outdoors, e.g. the woods, playpark + use a range of resources such as trikes.

> **Language-rich environment** An environment with a lot of talking and interaction between children and other people.

Relationships

Children who have strong relationships with other people have better social and emotional development. Children's relationships with adults, especially parents, play a very important part in their development.

Figure 2.2 shows why having positive relationships with adults is important.

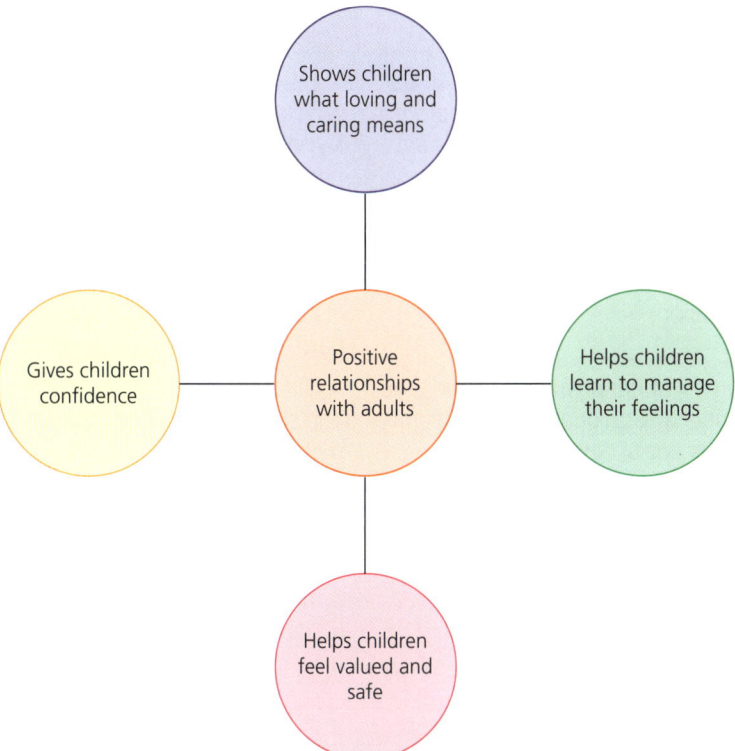

Figure 2.2 The effect of positive relationships with adults

Relationships with other children also matter. When children play together or are in a group, they learn how to be with others. Friendships with other children also help children to feel happy and confident.

> **Typical mistake**
>
> Don't forget that the relationships children have with each other can also be very important.

> **Check your understanding**
>
> 7 A child has a positive relationship with her mother. Explain how this might affect the child's emotional development.

2.3 Effects of biological and environmental factors

You will need to learn how biological and environmental factors can cause short- and long-term effects on a child's health and development.

> **Exam tip**
>
> Remember that the short- and long-term effects of environmental factors may be positive. For example, moving home may result in a family being able to keep a pet.

Short-term effects of biological factors

Five possible short-term effects of biological factors on a child's development are given in the specification: see Table 2.4.

Table 2.4 Possible short-term effects of biological factors

Short-term effect	Why	Example
Limited learning opportunities	Some biological factors might affect whether children can do things that are important for learning, such as listening or moving.	A child who has **Attention deficit hyperactivity disorder (ADHD)** might find it hard to sit and listen if the adults do not understand that she needs to learn in a different way.
Limited concentration when at a childcare setting	Some health conditions affect concentration.	A child who is not sleeping at night, for instance because of eczema, might find it hard to concentrate in nursery.
Withdrawn social behaviour/ **inhibited relationships** with others	Children might not be able to spend time with other children or adults. This might affect their social development.	A child is often absent because of illness. The child misses out on opportunities to make friends
Insecure parental attachment	Parents might find it hard to bond with a baby or child who is born early.	A baby who cries a lot because of a health condition might make it hard for a parent to bond, until the baby's health improves.
Secure parental attachment	Many babies and children develop good bonds with their parents or carers.	A mother has a set of twins and is supported to care for them. Both children have secure parental attachment.

Revision activity

Without looking at the information above, write a list of the five short-term effects that might be linked to biological factors. How many examples can you give?

Check your understanding

8 Identify **one** short-term effect on a child's development as a result of the child having a health condition.

> **Attention deficit hyperactivity disorder (ADHD)** A condition that means that children find it hard to sit and concentrate and therefore need to learn in different ways.
>
> **Inhibited relationships** When a child cannot trust others and therefore is not as close to others as they could be.

Long-term effects of biological factors

Long-term effects might affect children over a period of time and into adulthood. You need to learn the six effects in the specification.

Reduced educational attainment

Children might have reduced educational attainment because:
+ they have missed too much school
+ they find it hard to concentrate
+ they might not have had many learning opportunities.

Check your understanding

9 Explain why reduced educational attainment might happen.

> **Reduced educational attainment** Children not doing as well at school as they are able.

Limited range of career choices

Biological effects can affect a child's future career:
+ Some health conditions affect a person's stamina, strength or ability to do certain jobs.
+ Children might not have gained qualifications needed for certain careers because of health issues which caused them to be unwell and miss school.

Declining growth

Some inherited medical conditions affect the body's ability to grow and maintain cells. This can result in health that becomes worse over time.

Check your understanding and progress at www.hoddereducation.co.uk/myrevisionnotes

Mental illness
Mental illness can have a long-term effect on children.
+ Feeling different from others can cause children to lose confidence and develop anxiety and depression.
+ Some mental illness such as depression is linked to genetics.

Difficulty managing feelings
A child's emotional development can have long-term effects.
+ Children's emotional development might be affected by feeling different from others.
+ They might have missed out on being with other children if they were absent from school. This might mean that they have not learnt to develop some key social and emotional skills.
+ They might not have a strong attachment to their parents or other key adults.

Achieving/not achieving expected age-related milestones
Children might miss key milestones due to biological factors.
+ Young children with medical conditions might not meet their expected milestones.
+ They might have missed out on opportunities to talk, learn and explore.
+ Young children with learning difficulties might not meet their expected milestones for cognitive development.

> **Exam tip**
>
> Remember that a biological factor will probably cause more than one long-term effect.

Short-term effect of environmental factors on health and development
Six short-term effects of environmental factors are given in the specification.

Weight gain
Children might put on weight if:
+ they have a poor diet
+ they are not able to exercise much (some health conditions also affect this).

Illnesses and deficiencies
Environmental factors can affect a child's health.
+ Children might become ill or have deficiencies if they are not eating a healthy diet. A healthy diet includes vitamins and minerals that help children to grow strong and healthy. If vitamins or minerals are missing from their diet, they might find it harder to fight infections.
+ They might become ill if they are neglected or abused.
+ This might also happen if they live in poor housing which has, for example, mould. Breathing the air near mouldy surfaces can cause illness.

Positive feelings of wellbeing
Positive environmental factors affect children positively:
+ Children feel good if they have positive relationships with other people.
+ Children might feel positive if they have opportunities for stimulation, such as learning how to count things.
+ Children might feel positive if they have live in safe housing situations.

Meeting expected age-related milestones
Environmental factors can help children to meet milestones:
+ Children who have their basic needs met are likely to meet expected milestones.
+ Children who have opportunities for stimulation and exercise are more likely to meet the expected milestones.

Not meeting expected age-related milestones

This is the reverse of the above – if children do not have their basic needs met or opportunities for exercise/to be stimulated, they will not meet their milestones.

We saw in Chapter 1 that milestones are important because development follows a sequence. For example, if a child has not met the milestone for walking, they will not be able to meet the next milestones of climbing and running. This might happen if the child has not been able to play freely on the floor because the family has little space indoors.

Secure/insecure parental attachment

Children need positive time and physical affection from their parents. This in turn gives children emotional and social skills. Parents may not always be able to give time and affection to their children for a number of reasons. They might be depressed or stressed and/or they may have an addiction to alcohol or drugs.

Without positive time and physical affection, children might not develop social and emotional skills. They may show unwanted behaviours, or aggression, or become withdrawn. Insecure attachment might occur if children's basic needs are not met. Secure attachment is more likely if parents have a healthy lifestyle.

> **Check your understanding**
>
> 10 Match the short-term effect to the example. The first one has been done for you. For each short-term effect, can you think of another example of an environmental factor?
>
> | Short-term effect | Example |
> |---|---|
> | a. weight gain | 1. A child starts at a nursery and is given support with their physical development. |
> | b. positive feelings of wellbeing | 2. A parent becomes depressed and rarely talks to her baby. Her baby does not communicate much. |
> | c. illnesses and deficiencies | 3. A parent attends parenting classes and becomes more confident with their child. |
> | d. meeting expected age-related milestones | 4. A child's family pays for swimming lessons. The child has just learnt to swim and is very excited. |
> | e. not meeting expected age-related milestones | 5. Family goes on holiday and the child eats a lot of ice cream and pizza. |
> | f. secure parental attachment | 6. A homeless family is given short-term shelter in a flat that is cold and damp. The child develops a chest infection. |
>
> (a matches to 5)

Long-term effects of environmental factors on health and development

You will need to learn that children may have long-term effects on their health and development caused by environmental factors. These are listed in Table 2.5.

> **Exam tip**
>
> Remember that environmental factors could cause more than one long-term effect on a child's development.

Table 2.5 Long-term effects of environmental factors on development

Long-term effect	Link to environmental factor
Limited range of career choices	+ lack of stimulation and learning opportunities + low levels of confidence + basic needs have not been met
Thriving growth and healthy body weight	+ healthy diet + opportunities for exercise
Nutritional deficiency	+ unhealthy diet + neglect
Pain	+ physical abuse causing long-term injury
Successful educational achievement	+ opportunities for stimulation, interaction, and learning skills and concepts + positive relationships + opportunities for exercise + healthy diet + basic needs met + provision of education
Achieving expected milestones	+ opportunities for stimulation and interaction + positive relationships + opportunities for exercise + healthy diet + basic needs met
Not achieving expected milestones	+ basic needs unmet + lack of exercise + unhealthy diet + abuse + neglect + insecure attachment and poor relationships with others + lack of stimulation
Positive **emotional wellbeing**	+ positive relationships and secure attachment + opportunities for interaction + opportunities for stimulation

> **Emotional wellbeing** A state of good mental health.

> **Revision activity**
> Look at the short-term effects of environmental factors. Compare these to the long-term effects. Make a list of those effects that appear in both sections.

2.4 Transitions

REVISED

Transitions are significant for children. They involve a change of place, person or circumstance.

You will need to learn the different types of transitions that children might experience. You will also need to learn about the positive and negative effects of transitions on children.

> **Transition** The change from one stage or state to another.

> **Exam tip**
> You are likely to have a question about transitions in your exam. Make sure that you can identify expected and unexpected transitions. Revise carefully the various ways that transitions can affect children's development.

> **Exam tip**
> Make sure that you can define what a transition is and give an example of one.

2.4.1 Types of transitions

Transitions are either expected or unexpected.

Expected transitions

These are transitions that adults know will happen. They can prepare children for these. Seven examples of expected transitions are given in Figure 2.3, but there may be others.

Figure 2.3 Expected transitions

> **Revision activity**
>
> To help you learn the seven different transitions, you can group them into three categories: childcare changes, changes for the family and changes to care routines.
>
> Look at Figure 2.3 and complete this table.
>
> One category has been completed for you.
>
> | 1 | Childcare changes | |
> |---|---|---|
> | 2 | Changes for the family | + Planned hospital admission of themselves or a family member
+ Moving home
+ Birth of a sibling |
> | 3 | Changes to care routines | |

Unexpected transitions

Remember that an unexpected transition is one which is sudden for the child.

Table 2.6 shows three unexpected transitions. Note that the examples given are just to aid your understanding. The exam might contain a question with a different example in it.

> **Exam tip**
>
> If you are asked whether a transition is expected or not, think about whether adults would have time to prepare a child.

Table 2.6 Explaining unexpected transitions

Unexpected transition	Examples
Bereavement of a friend, family member or pet	+ Grandparent dies + Pet dog dies + A child or adult in the nursery dies
Change to **family dynamic**/circumstances	+ A parent loses their job + A parent goes back to work + A parent starts to abuse drugs
Family structure and separation	+ Parents split up + A parent's new partner moves in

> **Bereavement** The death of a person or pet.
>
> **Family dynamic** The way relationships work in a family.

Check your understanding and progress at www.hoddereducation.co.uk/myrevisionnotes

> **Revision activity**
>
> Look at this list of transitions:
> + A parent is in hospital because of an accident.
> + A child is starting to be cared for by a childminder.
> + A child's mother is pregnant.
> + A child's goldfish has died.
>
> Copy out this table and put each transition into the correct column.
>
> | Expected | Unexpected |
> |---|---|
> | | |

> **Check your understanding**
>
> 11 Jake is due to start at a new nursery because his family are moving. Jake's parents have split up, and Jake and his mother are staying with his grandfather.
> + Identify the different transitions that Jake is experiencing.
> + For each transition, decide whether it is expected or unexpected.

2.4.2 The impact of transitions on the child's development

There are many ways that transitions can affect children's health and development. The effects of transitions have been grouped into four areas:
+ Physical development
+ Cognitive development
+ Communication and language development
+ Social and emotional development.

> **Exam tip**
>
> Remember that children may be affected in more than one way by a transition.

Physical development

Children's health and physical development can be affected by transition. You need to learn the seven examples given:
+ loss of or increased appetite
+ sleeping patterns, nightmares
+ wetting/bedwetting
+ new fine and gross motor skills
+ regression or independence with self-care routines
+ ill health, vulnerability to chronic illnesses
+ access to new healthy food choices.

> **Regression** Aspects of a child's development may go backwards.
>
> **Vulnerability** Higher chance of something negative happening.
>
> **Chronic illness** A health problem that is either long-term or comes back repeatedly.

> **Check your understanding**
>
> 12 What does the term 'chronic' mean?

> **Revision activity**
>
> Look at the list of seven ways in which children's physical health and development might be affected. How many positive ways are there?
>
> For each positive way, give an example of why this might have happened.

Cognitive development

Cognitive development is about the ability to concentrate, learn and remember and also problem solve. Table 2.7 shows five effects of transition on a child's cognitive development.

Table 2.7 Effects of transition on a child's cognitive development

Impact	Explanation
Difficulty understanding the concept of change	A child might not understand what has happened and why. They may become confused.
Lack of concentration	A child might find it hard to concentrate because she is thinking about what has happened.
Learning from new experiences	A child may see or do new things and so will add to their knowledge.
Developing skills to deal with new challenges	Children might use problem solving to help them with the change in their life.
Affecting healthy brain development	+ Meeting new people and doing new things might help the brain develop. + Being afraid or not being able to concentrate might affect brain development.

Communication and language

Communication and language is about talking, listening and understanding others.

Four effects of transitions are given in this section: see Figure 2.4. Three are negative and one is positive.

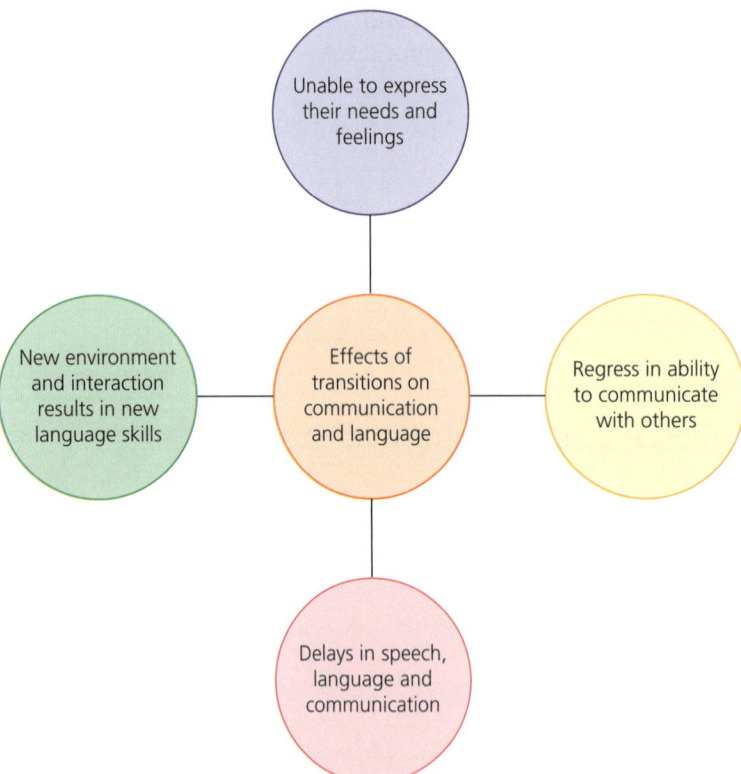

Figure 2.4 How communication and language can be affected by transitions

Social and emotional development

There are four aspects within social and emotional development to learn: see Table 2.8. For each area, you need to be able to give examples of impacts that transition will have.

Check your understanding and progress at www.hoddereducation.co.uk/myrevisionnotes

Table 2.8 Effects of transition on social and emotional development

Aspect	Examples
Showing strong feelings and emotions	+ Excitement + Sadness + Sense of loss + Fear + Anger + Withdrawal
Expressing emotions	+ Crying + Biting + Kicking + Being clingy + Regression, e.g. sucking fingers
Affecting emotional wellbeing	+ Levels of **resilience**: some children will gain confidence knowing that they can cope with new situations. Other children might learn to be fearful and so become less resilient. + The child may show signs of anxiety, e.g. clinging, crying or withdrawal.
Experiencing interaction with new role models (Communication with adults who model positive behaviours and language)	+ Children gain confidence to manage and cope with new feelings. + Children develop social skills as a result of being with a role model.

Revision activity

Copy out this table. For each area of development, give at least three effects from memory.

Now look at the information above to see how you did and the other effects you could have chosen.

Area	Effects of transition
Physical development	
Cognitive development	
Communication and language development	
Social and emotional development	
Emotional wellbeing	

Resilience Being able to cope with setbacks.

Exam tip

Always read and think about a case study carefully. There might be positive effects from a transition to think about, as well as negative effects.

2.5 Support strategies

REVISED

In this section, you will need to learn ways in which an adult can support children during transitions. This is important so that children's wellbeing and basic care needs are met.

This section can be revised in two parts:
1. Strategies to support the child and family during expected transitions.
2. Specific ways to support children before and during certain types of transitions.

Revision activity

See how many expected transitions you can write down in three minutes. Afterwards, check whether you missed any.

Strategies to support the child and family during expected transitions

You will need to learn the three main strategies to support the child and the family during transitions:
+ Build positive relationships with the child and family.
+ Adopt a child-centred approach.
+ Provide experiences for expression.

For each strategy, you must also learn what this means in practice.

Build positive relationships with the child and family

Early years practitioners will need to know how to build positive relationships with children and families.

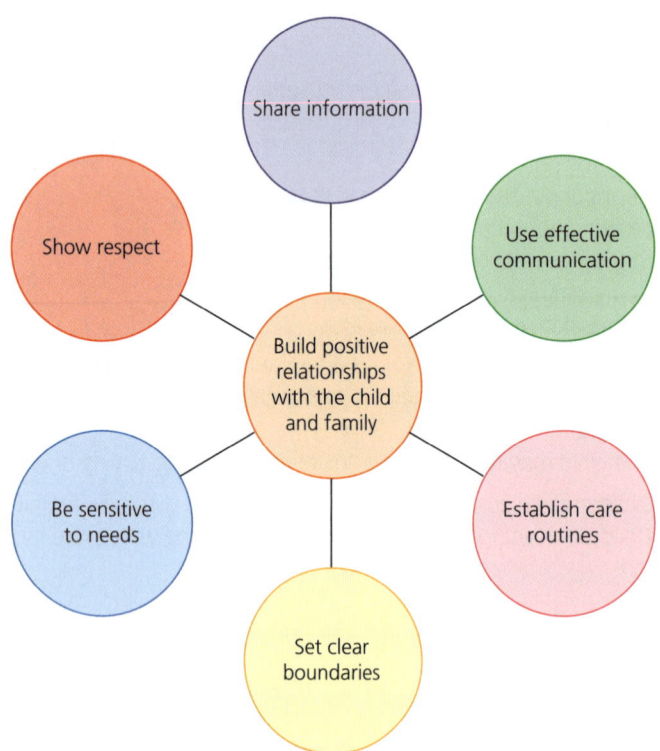

Figure 2.5 Ways to build positive relationships with the child and family

> **Revision activity**
>
> Look at the list of six ways shown in Figure 2.5 in which adults can build relationships with a child and their family.
>
> Choose three of the ways. For each one, give an example of how this might happen in practice. For example, 'A practitioner can share information by writing a note of what has happened each day.'

Adopt a child-centred approach

The term **child-centred approach** means making decisions based on children's interests and opinions but also on their needs.

You need to remember the three practical ways of showing a child-centred approach:
+ Have realistic expectations of the child's needs and interests.
+ Find out about the child's interests.
+ Maintain consistency in care.

> **Child-centred approach** Basing care decisions around a child's needs, interests and opinions.

> **Check your understanding**
>
> **13** True or false: A child-centred approach means allowing children do everything that they want.

Provide experiences for expression

Experiences for expression help children to show and talk about how they are feeling. Three examples need to be learnt for this section:
+ imaginative play
+ sensory experiences
+ sharing books with the child.

> **Revision activity**
>
> Can you think of one example of imaginative play and one example of a sensory experience? Share them with a partner.

Specific ways to support children during expected and unexpected transitions

As well as learning the strategies to support children for planned transitions, you also need to learn some of the ways that you can support the wellbeing and basic care of children before and during some specific transitions. Six specific transitions are given in Table 2.9.

Table 2.9 How to support children during transitions

Transition	How adults can support children during this transition
Starting a new childcare or education setting	+ Visits to the setting prior to starting can help the child adjust. + The keyworker visits the child at home to introduce themselves and explain what will happen. + Parents/carers can read books about starting school/setting. + Role play may be used to play 'schools'.
Birth of a new baby	+ Children can play with toy dolls and prams. + Parents can read books about the birth of a new baby. + It may help to visit a family who have a new baby. + The child can help choose toys or clothes for the new baby.
Planned hospital admission	+ The child could visit the hospital prior to admission. + They might watch a children's TV programme about a hospital. + They can use doctors' or nurses' costumes for dressing up and play. + Adults and children may look at the hospital website to see pictures of staff and facilities.
Bereavement of a friend or family member	+ Children might read books about bereavement. + They could create a memory box with special objects and photographs. + It can be helpful to sensitively talk about the person who has died.
Change to family circumstance/dynamic	+ Adults can create opportunities for discussion. + Families can create a family tree together. + Children can read books about different families.
Family structure and separation/attachment issues	+ Families may access help from professionals. + They can read books about the situation. + It is important to try to spend time together as a family.

Exam tip

It is highly likely that you will be asked a question about how to support a child going through a transition. Make sure that you have revised this carefully.

Check your understanding

14 Which of the transitions in Table 2.9 are unexpected transitions?

Revision activity

Fill in the missing bullet points in this table.

Afterwards check against Table 2.9 to see if your answers are correct.

Transition	How adults can support children during this transition
Starting a new childcare or education setting	+ Visits to the setting prior to starting. + Keyworker visits the child at home. + ? + ?
Birth of a new baby	+ Play with toy dolls and prams. + Read books about the birth of a new baby. + ? + Help choose toys or clothes for the new baby.
Planned hospital admission	+ ? + ? + Use doctors' or nurses' costumes for dressing up and play. + Look at the hospital website to see pictures of staff and facilities.
Bereavement of a friend or family member	+ Read books about bereavement. + ? + ?

Revision activity (Continued)

Transition	How adults can support children during this transition
Change to family circumstance/dynamic	+ Give opportunity for discussion. + ? + ?
Family structure and separation/attachment issues	+ Access help from professionals. + ? + ?

Exam-style questions

1. Which **one** of these is an expected transition?
   - A Starting school
   - B Death of a family pet
   - C Separation of parents
   - D Sudden illness of a parent [1]

2. Give **one** biological factor that might affect a child's development. [1]

3. Which **one** of the following is a biological factor in a child's development?
   - A A child's eye colour
   - B A child's favourite song
   - C A child's interest in dinosaurs
   - D A child's favourite colour [1]

4. State **one** strategy an early years practitioner can use to prepare a child for going into hospital. Explain how this strategy supports the transition of going to hospital. [3]

5. a) Give **two** environmental factors that might affect the development of a child. [2]
   b) Describe how **one** of the environmental factors given in your answer to 5a impacts the cognitive development of a child. [2]

6. A family is at a playground with their three-year-old. The parents play with and talk to their child. They help the child use some of the equipment.
   a) Identify whether this is an example of an environmental or biological factor. [1]
   b) Analyse how this activity might contribute to the child's development. [2]

7. Rasha is four years old. She has come to school in tears as her pet cat died last night.
   a) Identify whether this is an example of an expected or unexpected transition. [1]
   b) Explain **one** strategy that the school can use to help Rasha with this transition. [2]

8. Which **one** of the following strategies would best support a child starting school?
   - A Listening to a story
   - B Practising lining up
   - C Playing with dough
   - D Playing 'schools' in the role-play area [1]

9. Identify **two** ways in which a child's development might be affected as a result of living in a rural area. [2]

10. Evaluate the impact of a chronic medical condition on a child's long-term development. [6]

11. Evaluate how a child's overall development might be negatively affected by a sudden bereavement of a family member. [6]

12. A three-year-old child with delayed development has started at a nursery. The child's development is delayed as a result of neglect. The nursery is successful at supporting children who have difficulties. This child now has many opportunities to play and do activities with their key person, who is very good at supporting social and emotional development as well as language. The nursery provides healthy, freshly cooked food. It also works with parents and carers to provide them with information and resources to use at home.

    Analyse how the transition to the nursery may impact on this child's development. [6]

13. Ajay is two years old and goes to a childminder. His parents have just separated. Ajay is not yet talking fluently, which is typical in terms of development for his age.
    a) Explain why it is important that the childminder keeps in contact with Ajay's family. [1]
    b) State one way in which the childminder can help Ajay to express his feelings. [1]

14. Songul is four years old. She lives in a large house with her parents and grandparents. Her family talk to her and share books with her. She is a much-loved child. Songul is taken everywhere in the car or in a pushchair. She does not like playing outdoors. She loves baking and nearly every day her grandmother makes cakes and biscuits with her.

    Evaluate the short- and long-term impact on Songul's health and development of these environmental factors. [6]

Use your knowledge

Fenella is three years old. She has an inherited medical condition, which means that she often goes into hospital for tests or treatment. She lacks energy and is often out of breath. Fenella's family is very close. They spend a lot of time talking, going out on day trips and also sharing books with her. Fenella is due to go back into hospital next month for an extended stay. Her parents, the nursery and the hospital teaching service are working together to support Fenella. The nursery has sent the following assessment about Fenella's development to the hospital teaching service.

You have been asked by the teaching service to liaise with the nursery and Fenella's parents.

As a meeting is not possible, you have been asked to send in a report and also an action plan.

Your report should:
+ identify the strengths and weaknesses of Fenella's development using key milestones as a reference
+ explain the biological and environmental factors that might be impacting on Fenella's development
+ analyse how Fenella's development might be affected as a result of the transition into hospital.

Your action plan should provide practical strategies for supporting Fenella's transition into hospital and rationale for your suggestions.

Developmental assessment

Name: Fenella X
Age: 3 years 3 months

Date: 10/02/23
Completed by: J. Smith

Physical development	Communication and language
Fenella loves jigsaw puzzles and using crayons. Fenella is now showing an interest in using the tricycle, but is still learning to pedal and steer.	Fenella is able to use questions and form complicated sentences. She listens to long stories and can retell them afterwards. She loves looking at books and can pick out some words.
Cognitive development	**Social and emotional development**
Fenella is good at solving problems and also remembering things. She can sort objects into colours and shapes. She can recognise numbers to 20 and can do simple calculations.	Fenella is a confident and independent child. She loves being with her friends and plays very co-operatively with them. Fenella sometimes show signs of frustration and anger if she is tired, or cannot join in because she is tired.

Figure 2.6 Example of a developmental assessment

3 Care routines, play and activities to support the child

In this chapter, you will need to know about children's basic needs and the different ways in which early years settings can support them through the way in which they plan care routines, play and activities. You will also need to know about the early years practitioner's role before, during and after carrying out play activities.

3.1 Basic care needs

REVISED

Children's basic care and **psychological** needs are based on the theory of Maslow's Hierarchy of Needs. You will need to know about Maslow's theory and how this relates to basic human needs to see why early years practitioners plan routines and activities in a particular way.

You should also check that you are familiar with the term **physiological** and what this means when talking about basic needs.

> **Psychological** Relating to or affecting the mind.
>
> **Physiological** Related to the body, and the way in which living things work or what they need to survive (for example air, water, food, sleep, exercise and shelter).

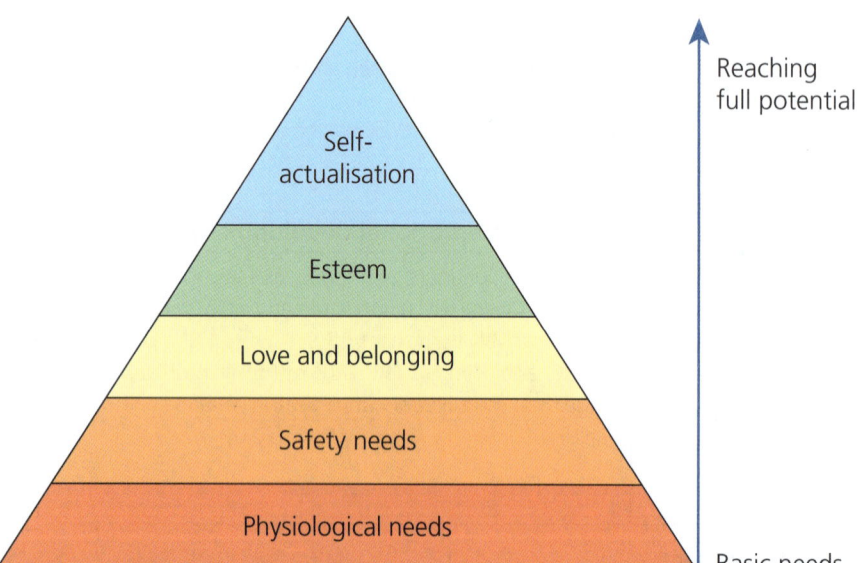

Figure 3.1 Maslow's hierarchy of needs

> **Revision activity**
>
> Draw a version of Maslow's triangle, making sure you have written the different stages on it. Then check that you have learnt each of the levels and what they mean.
> + Cut up the triangle and write what each stage means on the back of each piece.
> + Test a partner on the different stages.

Basic needs

The following basic needs relate directly to what Maslow meant by physiological needs. You can also see from Table 3.1 what they mean for the role of the early years practitioner. You will need to be able to give examples of each of them.

Table 3.1 How children's basic needs can be met by adults

Basic need	How the need can be met by adults
Food and drink	+ Provide healthy daily snacks. + Give access to drinking water.
Fresh air	+ Plan regular opportunities for outdoor play. + Provide trips outside the setting.
Rest and sleep	+ Make available quiet activities. + Schedule nap times.
Exercise	+ Provide access to climbing equipment. + Offer times for physical movement (e.g. dance).
Physical safety	+ Check equipment regularly for faults. + Make sure doors and gates are locked (except emergency exits). + Never use physical punishment.
Emotional safety	+ Provide a consistent keyworker for each child. + Establish keyworker interaction. + Arrange small group play. + Be a caring practitioner. + Ensure bullying is not tolerated.
Shelter	+ Provide a warm and welcoming environment. + Provide areas shaded from the sun.

> **Check your understanding**
>
> 1 Seven basic needs are listed in Table 3.1. Write down the ways in which an early years practitioner provides support for children's physical and emotional safety. You can do the same for the other basic needs.

Psychological needs

Children's psychological needs are more abstract than their basic needs, and relate to their thoughts and feelings. They are closer to the top of Maslow's pyramid and are to do with to children's confidence, sense of belonging and self-esteem.

Table 3.2 How children's psychological needs can be met by adults

Psychological need	How the need can be met by adults
Belonging	+ Respond to the child's interests. + Encourage the child to join in. + Provide opportunities to interact with others.
Affection	+ Comfort a child when distressed. + Show empathy.
Sense of achievement	+ Praise the child's efforts. + Recognise positive behaviour.
Being valued	+ Display the child's artwork. + Show an interest in the child's culture. + Listen attentively to the child. + Recognise their needs.
Establishing emotional boundaries	+ Provide consistency with rules. + Help children to understand why rules are important.

> **Check your understanding**
>
> 2 What is meant by psychological needs? Why are they important?

> **Typical mistake**
>
> Remember the difference between the words physiological and psychological. One way of remembering is that physs- sounds like 'fizzy' or being alive, and psycho- is to do with feelings.

3.2 Basic care routines and play activities to support the child's development

REVISED

The basic care routines and activities which take place in early years settings are all opportunities to support children's development. This is because they promote each child's independence, health, safety and wellbeing.

3.2.1 Basic care routines

Children enjoy having routines during the day as they help to build their confidence. This is because through routines they will start to learn what will happen next. For example, 'If we have just had a story, that means we are going home soon.' Care routines should be built into the day and will also gradually help children to learn basic self-care as they will be repeated regularly.

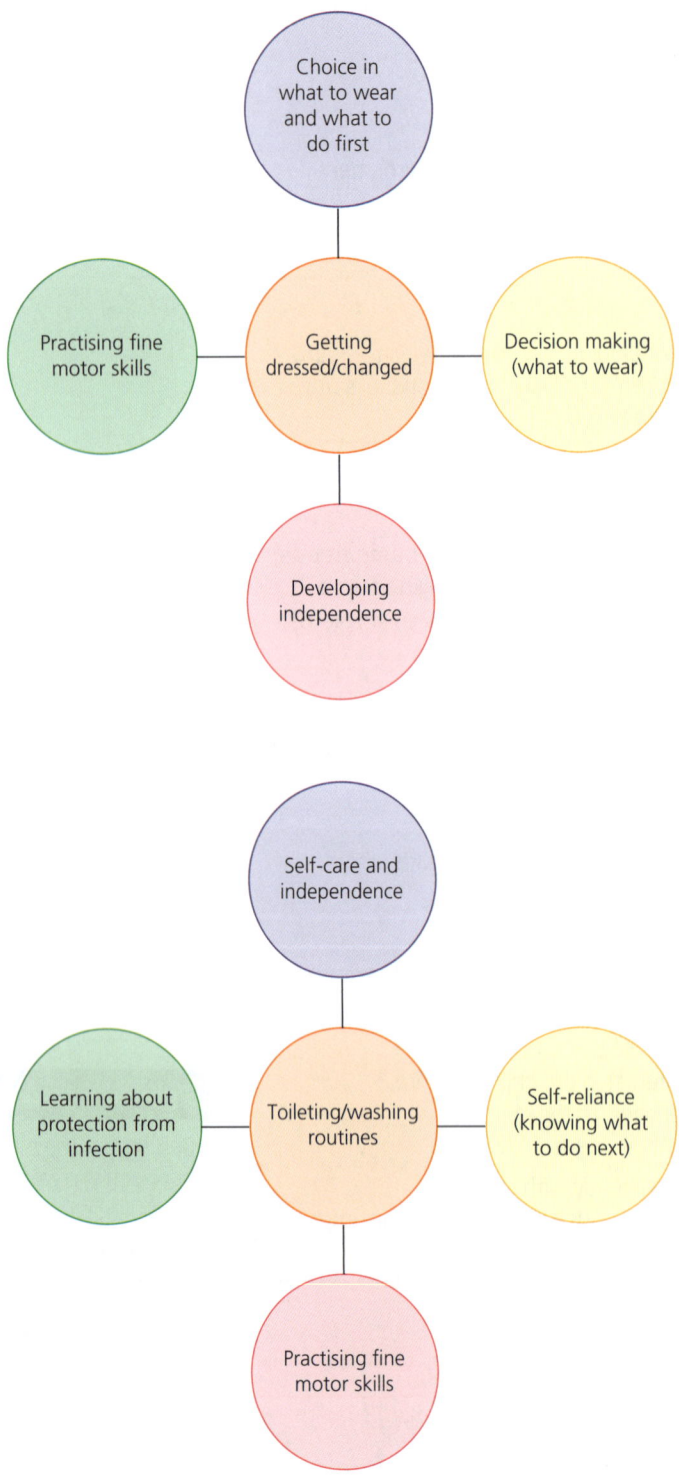

Check your understanding and progress at www.hoddereducation.co.uk/myrevisionnotes

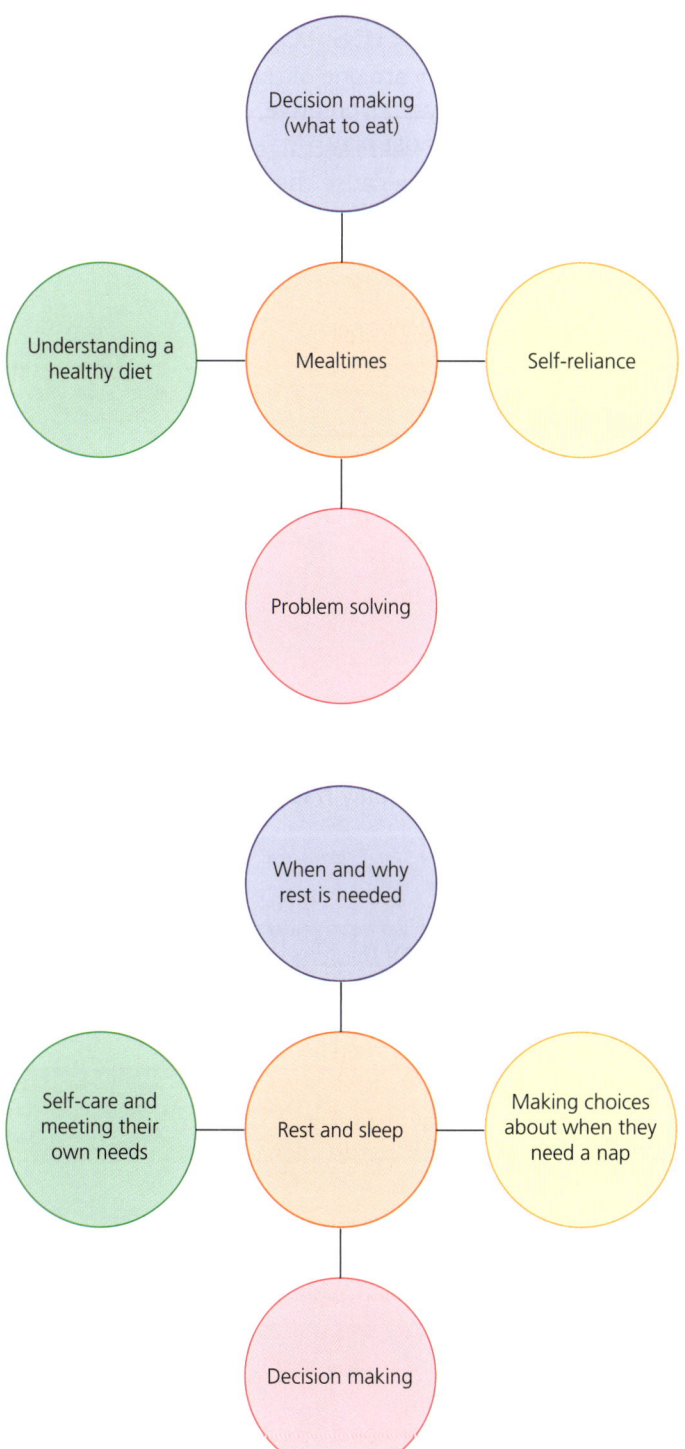

Figure 3.2 Why care routines are important for children's independence, health, safety and wellbeing

Check your understanding

3. How does the activity of getting dressed help a child to learn independence?

Revision activity

Using the spider diagrams in Figure 3.2, ask someone to test you about each of the four care routines and why they are important for children's development.

3.2.2 Play activities

Play activities are important for children's development as they are one of the ways in which they learn. This may be through a focus on physical, creative, imaginative or sensory play. You should also remember that most play activities are holistic, and can support all areas of development.

You will need to be able to give examples of each of the different types of play and the kinds of resources that may be needed for each.

> **Sensory play** A type of play which encourages children to learn using their senses. Some examples include using dough or water, or making shakers.

> **Exam tip**
>
> You will need to remember the names of the four different types of play. It may help you to use the acronym SCIP:
> - **S**ensory
> - **C**reative
> - **I**maginative
> - **P**hysical.

Physical play

This is any kind of play which involves physical activity. Physical play has benefits for children in different areas, as shown in Table 3.3.

Table 3.3 Benefits of physical play

Benefits of physical play	This encourages children to:
Balance and co-ordination	Use their gross motor skills: running and jumping, throwing and catching, hopping and skipping, climbing, using scooters and pedal toys.
Control of fine movements	Use their fine motor skills: clay and dough, mark making, threading beads, construction toys, using a spoon.
New concepts	Explore their physical environment safely and understand their place in it.
Confidence	Develop their confidence and self-esteem as they learn about risk and challenge as well as how to plan activities safely.
Healthy wellbeing	Develop their physical strength. Learn to play together and think about others, which supports social and emotional development and mental wellbeing.

> **Revision activity**
>
> Using the format of a spider diagram with the words 'physical play' in the centre, draw a diagram to show how it benefits children in different areas.

Figure 3.3 What are the benefits of physical play in the outdoor environment?

Creative play

This type of play encourages children to explore and experiment using a range of different media. It should be as child-centred as possible rather than driven by adults towards a specific end result.

> **Media** Different ways in which creativity is expressed, for example painting, drawing or music.
>
> **Child-centred** Putting the needs of the child first and encouraging them to be independent.

Table 3.4 Benefits of creative play

Benefits of creative play	It encourages children to:
New language	+ Use different materials and media. + Introduce new vocabulary, for example when talking about how music makes them feel or when exploring the texture of different materials.
New concepts	+ Use opportunities to explore new ideas, for example being creative with natural materials or junk modelling, or by using media in an unusual way.
Confidence	+ Explore their own ideas using different media will help to develop children's confidence. + Seeing displays in the setting including their work will support children's self-esteem.
Problem solving	+ Approach different tasks and solve problems. + Work with others and develop their speaking and listening skills as they talk through different ideas.

> **Revision activity**
>
> Write down the four benefits of creative play on separate pieces of paper.
> + On the back of each, write how the benefit supports children's development.
> + Test yourself to see if you can identify the benefits by reading how it supports children's development.
> + Then test yourself by choosing a benefit and explaining how it supports development.

> **Typical mistake**
>
> Make sure you understand the use of the word 'media'. In this context, it means ways of doing something creative.

> **Check your understanding**
>
> 4 Describe a creative activity using clay or dough with children and how this might benefit their development.

Imaginative play

Imaginative play gives children opportunities to picture and explore different scenarios in a safe environment.

Table 3.5 Benefits of imaginative play

Benefits of imaginative play	It encourages children to:
Expression of feelings	+ Think about their own feelings as well as those of others. + Put themselves in different situations and take on the role of other people or characters, for example in role play or when using dolls or small figures.
Control of fine motor skills	+ Use a range of fine motor skills. These include fastening dressing-up clothes, mark making and using puppets.
Relationships and communication	+ Children will need to co-operate with one another and share ideas.

> **Check your understanding**
>
> 5 List **three** types of imaginative play.

Sensory play

Sensory play gives children opportunities to use and explore their senses in different ways.

Table 3.6 Benefits of sensory play

Benefits of sensory play	It encourages children to:
Expression of feelings	+ Use sensory play to show how they feel, for example squeezing and exploring different materials, or playing a musical instrument.
Hand–eye co-ordination	+ Work on their hand–eye co-ordination as they look at and explore different resources such as slime or dough.
New concepts	+ Explore new concepts, for example through adding water to sand or adding paint to shaving foam. (Care should be taken to ensure that the substances provided can be safely mixed together.)
Concentration	+ Concentrate for longer periods as they explore new concepts such as the sensation of a mixture of cornflour and water.

> **Revision activity**
>
> Create a poster for parents showing the benefits of sensory play and how it supports different aspects of a child's development.

> **Check your understanding**
>
> 6 What do you understand by sensory play? What kinds of resources and materials might practitioners provide for children?

> **Exam tip**
>
> Remember that play activities might take place indoors or outdoors. Many of them can take place in either environment.

Check your understanding and progress at www.hoddereducation.co.uk/myrevisionnotes

3.3 The role of the early years practitioner during play activities

REVISED

You will need to know about and understand your role before, during and after supporting play activities with children. This means being well prepared for them as well as having clear routines in place in your setting.

Before play activities

Preparation is very important before starting play activities. Early years practitioners will need to ensure they have completed the following:

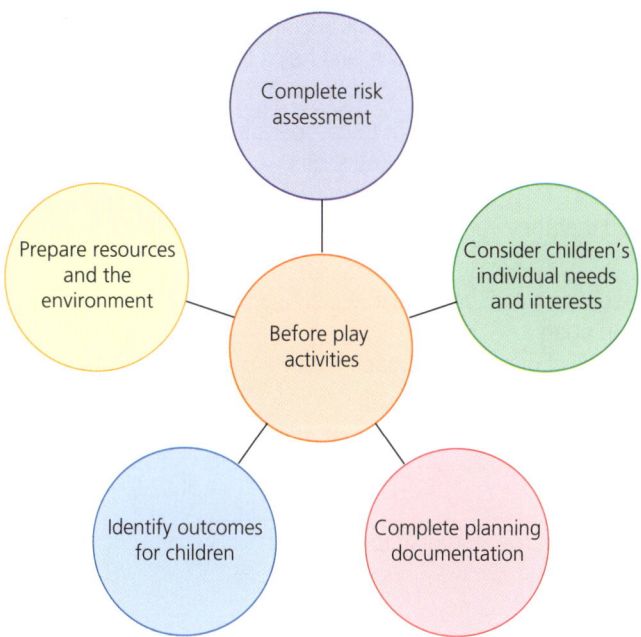

Figure 3.4 The role of the practitioner before play activities

You will need to know about **risk assessments** as all early years providers are required by law to make sure the environment is safe and fit for purpose. On a daily basis, this means:

+ doing a 'safety sweep' – checking that the environment is safe for children to use before activities
+ taking action to make it safe if necessary.

When preparing indoor or outdoor environments, practitioners should consider children's individual needs and interests, and ensure that they have access to a range of suitable resources.

> **Risk assessment** A process to identify existing or potential hazards, and to consider the risk of harm.

Check your understanding

7 What is meant by considering children's individual needs and interests?

Before play activities, practitioners will also need to complete the relevant planning paperwork. This sets out what is going to happen and when, and also helps everyone to see what resources will be needed.

Identifying outcomes for children is important at this stage. This means thinking in advance about what children should be able to do when they have completed an activity. For example, throwing a dice, looking at the dots and being able to match them to the correct numeral.

The resources and the environment also need to be prepared. This involves checking that there are enough resources for the children who will be doing the activity, for example:

+ If they will be painting, check that there are enough aprons.
+ Does the environment meet health and safety requirements? (See page 66–7.)

> **Exam tip**
>
> Make sure you know the difference between long-term, medium-term and short-term planning documents.

During play activities

Early years practitioners will need to provide support to children in different ways during play activities.

Table 3.7 How to provide support during play activities

Method of support	How to provide this support
Engage in **open-ended talk**	+ Make sure children are encouraged to talk about their ideas through the use of open-ended questions.
Provide praise and encouragement	+ Ensure praise and encouragement are given regularly. This is particularly important for young children and those that lack confidence.
Focus on interaction to support outcomes	+ Talk to children about what is happening; this also supports their speaking and listening skills, and helps to **scaffold** their learning.
Encourage socialisation and co-operation	+ Encourage children to socialise and learn to co-operate with one another as they might have limited social experiences. + Support children so that they can understand others' point of view.
Facilitate problem solving	+ Support problem-solving activities through encouraging discussion between peers. + Ask children questions about their approach if they are finding something challenging.
Listen to children's ideas	+ Always listen to children and talk to them about their ideas. This supports their self-esteem and helps us to understand their thoughts.
Manage children's safety	+ Be aware of potential hazards, and plan to reduce or avoid them. + Encourage children to do the same.
Promote independence	+ Support children in doing things for themselves as far as possible.
Manage behaviour	+ Support children through disagreements by talking through each side with them. + Asking the child to consider the impact of their actions on others.
Adapt activities, interaction or resources to ensure inclusion	+ Make sure all children are able to access all activities. + Adapt the method of communication where needed, for example using a Makaton to support a child with learning difficulties. + Adapt activities and resources if necessary, for instance if a child has additional needs or access requirements.

> **Open-ended talk** Questions and conversations which do not have a 'yes' or 'no' answer.
>
> **Scaffold** Provide support for learning by breaking it into smaller steps.

Revision activity

Write down or discuss with a partner some examples of how you could provide support in the following situations:
+ working with an autistic child who is very sensitive to noise
+ managing a disagreement between two children who both want to use the same tricycle
+ telling children that it is time to get ready to go home
+ encouraging children to think about safety when they are in the outside area
+ supporting children to set up a vet's surgery in the role-play area.

Check your understanding

8 What is meant by 'open-ended talk', and how can practitioners ensure that they do this?

Check your understanding and progress at www.hoddereducation.co.uk/myrevisionnotes

After play activities

After play activities, early years practitioners will need to do the following:

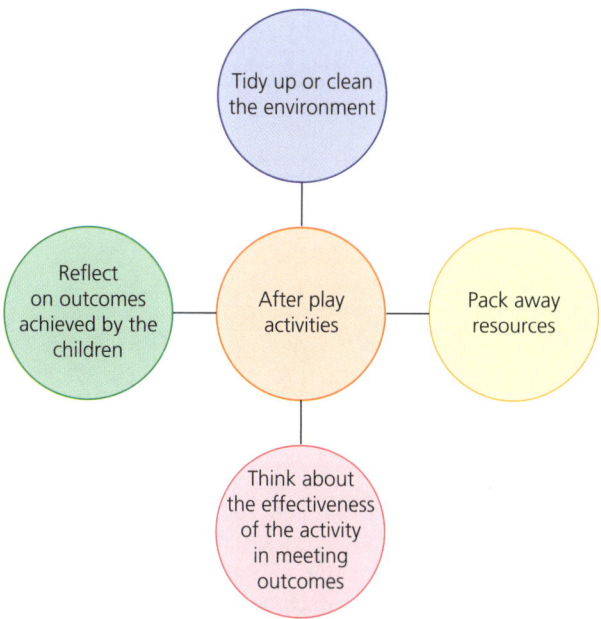

Figure 3.5 A practitioner's role after play activities

After each play activity, practitioners will need to think about how effective it has been and whether children have met learning outcomes. This helps them to think about whether they might repeat the activity or change it slightly if it is carried out again in the future.

Check your understanding

9   Why is it important for early years practitioners to think about what outcomes children have achieved after each activity?

Revision activity

Look at these activities:
+ Complete risk assessment.
+ Manage children's safety.
+ Tidy up/clean the environment.
+ Reflect on outcomes achieved by the children.
+ Promote independence.
+ Manage behaviour.
+ Complete planning documentation.
+ Encourage socialisation and co-operation.
+ Prepare resources and the environment.
+ Adapt activities, interaction or resources to ensure inclusion.
+ Provide praise and encouragement.
+ Think about the effectiveness of the activity.

Copy out this table. Thinking about your role, decide which column each of these activities should be in. The first three have been done for you.

Before play activities	During play activities	After play activities
Complete risk assessment.	Manage children's safety.	Tidy up/clean the environment.

Revision activity

The next time you carry out an activity with children, think carefully about the support that you give them before, during and afterwards. Tick off each of the points in Figures 3.4 and 3.5 and Table 3.7 as you do so, and see how many you carry out as part of your routine.

Exam-style questions

1. Which **one** of these is an example of a care routine?
   A Setting out learning activities
   B Reading to children
   C Rest and sleep
   D Home time [1]

2. Explain the importance of early years practitioners meeting the basic and psychological needs of children. [6]

3. An early years practitioner has asked some three- and four-year-olds to help her to lay the table ready for lunch. Explain how this process will support the children's development in different ways. [6]

4. Which **one** of the following is not an example of physical play?
   A Riding bicycles
   B Using dough
   C Listening to a story with an adult
   D Using construction toys [1]

5. State **one** way in which imaginative play benefits children. Explain how it does this. [3]

6. You have been asked to carry out a risk assessment in the learning environment. The outside area has several hazards (recorded in the left-hand column of the following table).

   Complete the rest of the table. [6]

Hazard	Who might be harmed and how?	Action needed to control the risk
Broken gate		
Bright sunlight/very warm		
Animal faeces in play area		

7. Mari is five years old and has a moderate hearing impairment. You notice that she wants to play in the construction area but that she is reluctant to approach the other children and has turned to you for support. Explain how this could impact on Mari if you do not take action. [3]

8. An early years setting has not carried out a safety check in three weeks due to staff illness. Explain how this might impact on safety in the setting. [3]

9. Hamza is three years old and regularly falls asleep during the day. Both of his parents work full-time. He arrives at the setting at 7 a.m. and is collected at 6 p.m. What can the setting do to ensure Hamza has enough rest and sleep, and why is this important? [3]

10. Choose three activities which support the development of fine motor skills. For each activity, explain **one** way it supports a child's development. [6]

Use your knowledge

Rhodri is two-and-a-half years old and has just started to be cared for by a new childminder. His parents have filled in the childminder's New Parent Information Form.

The childminder can see from the form and from Rhodri's limited time in the setting that Rhodri's physical skills are less developed than is usually expected for his age. When she carries out his two-year check, she finds that he has difficulty with his upper body strength in activities such as throwing a ball, and also lacks confidence when using trikes and scooters. He also finds it a challenge when using his fine motor skills.

Thinking about Rhodri's developmental needs, write a detailed plan to show what the childminder could do to support Rhodri within the setting during care routines and how the care routines will help to develop his:
+ basic needs
+ psychological needs
+ physical skills.

Check your understanding and progress at www.hoddereducation.co.uk/myrevisionnotes

4 Early years provision

This chapter looks at how education and care is provided for young children. You will need to learn about the purpose of early years provision, the different types and the ways in which it can vary.

4.1 Types of early years provision

REVISED

You will need to learn that there are three types of early years provision – see Table 4.1. The main difference between them is about how they are funded, whether they make a profit and how this profit is spent.

Table 4.1 Different types of early years provision

Type of provision	How it is organised	Examples
Statutory	This is provided in statute (required by law) and funded by the government. Statutory provision is often organised by the local authority.	A reception class
Private	These are profit-making businesses where services are chargeable (charged for).	Childminders, day nurseries and leisure activities such as swimming lessons
Voluntary and not-for-profit organisations	These are set up to meet the needs of children and their families. Organisations might charge but only to cover their costs. They may be run by charities, but also by parents and religious organisations.	A pre-school organised mainly by parents

> **Exam tip**
>
> Make sure that you can give an example of each of the different types of early years provision. There may be a multiple choice question on this.

Statutory Required by law and funded by the government.

Private Profit-making business where services are chargeable.

Voluntary Charities and not-for-profit organisations set up to meet the needs of children and their families.

> **Revision activity**
>
> Complete the table by remembering the points included in Table 4.1. Fill in the blanks.
>
> | Type of provision | How it is organised | Example |
> | --- | --- | --- |
> | Statutory | | |
> | | | Swimming lessons |
> | | Set up to meet the needs of children and their families | |

4.2 The purpose of early years provision

REVISED

There are many benefits when children go to early years settings. Children should benefit, but so too can parents and carers. You will need to know the three broad reasons for early years provision, with examples:
+ promotes holistic development
+ supports parents and carers
+ supports children's progress within the Early Years Stage Framework (EYFS).

Promotes holistic development

The activities, resources and knowledge of the staff in an early years setting should be designed to help children's overall development. You will need to know how early years provision can support children in each of these areas of development:

+ physical
+ cognitive
+ social and emotional
+ language and communication.

Figure 4.1 How do activities like this help children's holistic development?

Table 4.2 gives examples of how children's development can be promoted in each of the different areas.

Table 4.2 Promoting children's development

Area of development	Activities, equipment and resources	Support from staff
Physical	Balls, climbing frames, wheeled toys, construction toys, jigsaws, scissors, rolling pins, dough, sand, water	+ Choose the right equipment for the stage of development. + Teach children how to use tools and equipment. + Build children's confidence to use equipment.
Cognitive	Jigsaw puzzles, shape sorters, construction toys, number lines, different sizes of containers	+ Use mathematical language such as 'larger' or 'hexagon'. + Encourage children to problem solve. + Counting games and drawing children's attention to colour and shape.
Social and emotional	+ Activities that involve sharing, e.g. playing board games + Activities to express feelings, e.g. painting, playing musical instruments	+ Opportunities to talk about feelings and emotions. + Staff help children to take turns, share and be in small groups.
Language and communication	Role-play areas, books and stories, listening games	+ Introduce new words. + Share stories and rhymes.

Check your understanding

1 What does the term 'holistic' mean? (If you are not sure, look back at Chapter 1.)

Typical mistake

Don't write about only one area of development when a question uses the term 'holistic development'.

Check your understanding and progress at www.hoddereducation.co.uk/myrevisionnotes

> **Revision activity**
> Copy the spider diagram in Figure 4.2. Write a different area of development in each circle. Add a practical example of how each area of development may be promoted in early years provision.
>
>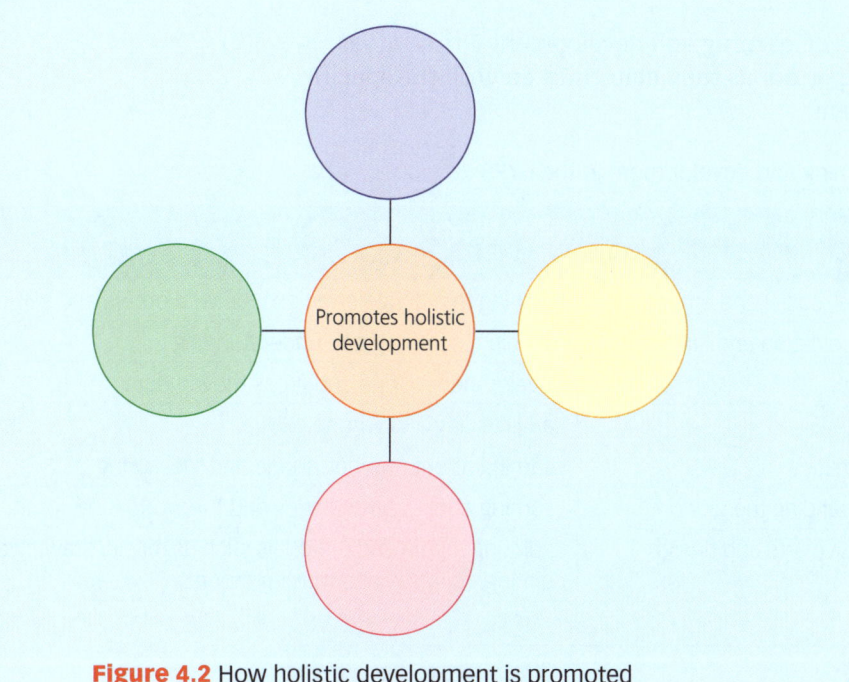
>
> **Figure 4.2** How holistic development is promoted

Supports parents or carers

Parents and carers can benefit when their children are in early years provision. You need to learn the four examples of how this might happen:
- Seek or retain employment – parents/carers are freed up to either work or look for work while their child is being cared for in the setting.
- Receive respite – parents/carers who have children with additional needs or caring responsibilities can have time off, knowing that their children are safe and happy.
- Access training opportunities – parents/carers may use the time to study for qualifications or do training to help them with their career. For instance, they might attend university or college.
- Participate in recreation and leisure activities – parents/carers might use the time for hobbies, exercise and leisure.

> **Revision activity**
> From memory, write down three ways that parents may use the time they have when their children are in early years provision.
>
> Compare your answers with the information here and note down the fourth way.

Promote learning to meet the early years learning goals within the EYFS

Early years provision can help children make progress with the statutory EYFS. To answer any questions about this, you will need to learn the following information about the EYFS:
- The EYFS covers all children from birth to five years old in England.
- Nearly all early years settings (including childminders but not Montessori settings or some private schools) are required by law to follow this framework, including reception classes.
- The framework includes a section that provides learning and development requirements.
- Seven areas of learning and development are given within the learning and development requirements. They are divided into prime and specific areas (see page 54).
- Goals are set for each of the areas of learning and development. These are called early learning goals.
- At the end of their reception year in school, children are assessed on whether they have met the goals in each of the seven areas.

> **Check your understanding**
>
> 2 a) How many areas of learning and development are there?
>   b) When are children assessed to see if they have met the early learning goals?

Table 4.3 shows the seven areas of learning and development. Prime areas are thought to be especially important as they help children with the specific areas of leaning and development.

Table 4.3 The seven areas of learning and development in the EYFS

Prime or specific	Area of learning and development	What they cover
Prime areas	Personal, social and emotional	Learning to manage emotions, be with others and self-care
	Communication and language	Listening, speaking and understanding
	Physical	Development of fine and gross movements
Specific areas	Literacy	Early reading and writing
	Mathematics	Learning about number, shape and measuring
	Understanding the world	Learning about communities and the world they live in
	Expressive arts and design	Exploring media and materials such as music, drawing and painting, role play and making models

> **Check your understanding**
>
> 3 What are the **three** prime areas of learning and development?

> **Revision activity**
>
> Try to memorise the information in Table 4.3, then copy and complete this table, adding the missing information.
>
> | Prime or specific | Area of learning and development | What they cover |
> |---|---|---|
> | Prime areas | Personal, social and emotional | |
> | | Communication and language | |
> | | Physical | |
> | Specific areas | Literacy | |
> | | Mathematics | |
> | | Understanding the world | |
> | | Expressive arts and design | |

Being in early years provision can help children make progress towards the early learning goals. This is because activities, resources and the way that staff work meet the requirements of the EYFS. An example of this is the way that children have opportunities to go on outings or have visitors in the setting, as this is a requirement of the specific area 'Understanding the world'.

4.3 Types of early years setting

REVISED

In section 4.1 we saw that early years provision can be funded and organised in three ways. In this section, you need to learn that there are also different types of early years settings.

Table 4.4 Different types of early years settings

Type of early years setting	Key points
Crèche	+ The parent/carer stays in the same building as the child. + A child up to the age of 8 is cared for during the day for a short period of time, regularly or occasionally.
Childminder	+ This is a person who looks after children of any age in the childminder's own home. + Care is provided during the school day, before or after school and during school holidays.
Nursery	+ Children aged 0–5 years attend the nursery for all or part of the day. + The setting is usually open for the full calendar year and provides care before and after school, and holiday care for older children.
Pre-school	+ Children aged 2–4 attend pre-school, which is often located in community venues. + Children may attend for a few hours or a full day during the school term.
Nursery class	+ Children aged 3–4 years attend a nursery class often connected to a primary school. + Children may attend for a morning or afternoon session or a full day during the school term, depending on circumstances.
Primary school	+ Legally children must attend from the term after their 5th birthday, but many children start primary school in the September of the year that they become 5 years old. + Children attend for school hours during term time. + The setting provides (sometimes in partnership with others) additional childcare outside school hours.

> **Check your understanding**
>
> 4 a) Which type of early years setting may be connected to a primary school?
>   b) Which early years setting is based in a home?

> **Revision activity**
>
> Using six cards, write a type of setting on each one. On the back of each card, copy out the key features of the setting.
> + Put the cards into a pile with the features face up.
> + Take a card, read the features and decide which setting it is describing.
> + Check whether you are right.
> + Repeat this, but looking at the other side of the cards (type of setting face up).

> **Typical mistake**
>
> Remember to include childminders in the types of provision that are available.

4.4 Variation in early years provision

REVISED

Every early years setting is slightly different. The differences between settings might affect the choices that parents and carers make. You will need to know the things that make them different.

There are four overall ways in which settings may vary:
+ accessibility
+ capacity
+ facilities
+ approach.

> **Exam tip**
>
> As well as learning the overall ways in which settings vary, you will need to know the specific examples and how they might affect parents' or carers' options and choices.

Accessibility

Cost

Parents' and carers' choices and options will be affected by whether an early years setting charges fees and how much these are.

Eligibility and admissions criteria

Some settings are set up to meet the needs of certain children and families. To make sure that the spaces are available for these children and families, they may set eligibility and admissions criteria. Examples include family income or whether a child has a special educational need and/or a disability.

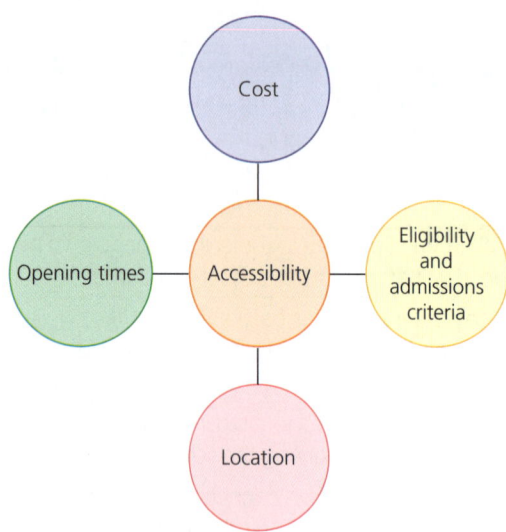

Figure 4.3 Accessibility issues affecting choice of setting

Location and opening times

Parents and carers need to think about how easily they can get to an early years setting from their home or work, as well as the opening times.

+ For parents/carers who work long hours, they might find that the opening hours of some settings do not match their work hours.
+ Parents/carers who do not drive might not be able to rely on public transport to reach the setting.

> **Check your understanding**
>
> 5 Why might working parents focus on opening hours when choosing an early years setting?

Capacity

This is about the number of children that a setting can take and also how many staff are available to work with children.

+ Parents might choose a setting with a high ratio of staff to children because the children will receive more attention and opportunities.
+ Some parents/carers choose early years settings or providers such as childminders that have few children, as they want their child in a setting with a more 'family' feel.

Maximum numbers of children for each setting and minimum staff ratios are set by the Department for Education.

Facilities

The space, layout and equipment can vary between early years settings.

Indoor environment

Here are some examples of how indoor environments may vary:
+ space available
+ layout of the rooms and buildings
+ furniture and equipment
+ lighting and decoration.

> **Exam tip**
>
> When answering a question about facilities, remember that these include the outdoor environment as well as the indoors.

Check your understanding and progress at www.hoddereducation.co.uk/myrevisionnotes

Indoor environments vary according to the type of provision. For example:
+ Where a setting takes many children of different ages, they will need more space and the setting may have separate areas for each age group. Some parents/carers will like this approach, but others may not.
+ A childminder may have less space but will take fewer children. Their provision will be homely. This will appeal to some parents/carers.
+ Some early years provision, such as pre-schools and crèches, is based in buildings owned by others, such as community centres, and therefore may not be able to choose the lighting, decoration or other aspects of the indoor environment.

Outdoor environment

Here are some ways that the outdoor environment may vary:
+ space available
+ surfaces, e.g. tarmac, grass, wood chippings
+ equipment such as climbing frames, large sand trays
+ landscaping, e.g. garden spaces, paths.

Figure 4.4 The outdoor environment promotes learning

Parents/carers who want their child to spend a lot of time playing outdoors might choose a setting that has a large outdoor space with lots for children to see and do.

Resources

The toys and smaller items in the indoor and outdoor environment can also vary. Some settings focus on natural resources such as wooden toys.

The resources that are available in a setting might help parents/carers to decide which setting to choose.
+ One family might want to see a lot of books in a setting.
+ Another family might want to see resources for painting or making things.

Approach

Some early years settings have a particular approach to working with children and their families. This can affect how they organise learning activities and draw up their policies and procedures.

Learning activities

What children do in a setting depends on how learning activities are planned. Here are some examples of how the approach to learning activities may vary. In a given setting, it may be the case that:
+ Most learning activities are planned for outdoors.
+ Learning activities are organised and led mainly by adults (adult-led).
+ Learning activities are chosen and led by children (child-led).
+ There is a focus on science and mathematics or literacy activities.
+ The setting focuses on creative activities such as paint, collage and construction.

Parents/carers might make a decision on the basis of these approaches.
+ Some parents/carers might want their children to be in a setting that is more 'child-led' as they want their children to spend more time playing freely.
+ Other parents/carers might want their children to learn to count and read during the early years, and so might choose a setting that focuses more on this.

Policies and procedures

There are legal requirements for early years settings to have certain policies and procedures such as those to do with health and safety (see Chapter 5). But settings might also have other policies which vary, such as how they settle children in and whether or not parents and carers can come inside the setting.

> **Exam tip**
>
> Make sure that when you give variations of provision, any examples you give are appropriate to the type of setting. For example, a nursery class will not take babies.

> **Check your understanding**
>
> 6 Why might the policies and procedures of an early years setting affect a parent's or carer's decision to use it?

> **Revision activity**
>
> Early years settings vary in what they provide.
>
> Fill in this table to show examples of how they vary. Then check back through the previous pages and see what you have missed.
>
> | Provided by settings | Examples |
> |---|---|
> | Accessibility | ?
 ?
 Location
 Opening times |
> | Capacity | ?
 ? |
> | Facilities | Indoor environment
 Outdoor environment
 ? |
> | Approach | ?
 _____ and _____ |

Exam-style questions

1. A reception class is an example of what type of provision? [1]

2. Discuss how attending an early years setting might support a child's holistic development. [6]

3. Felicity is a single mother who also cares part-time for her disabled brother. She has one daughter aged three years. Her daughter has now started at a local pre-school. Felicity is often tired and quite lonely. Her doctor has also said that she needs to exercise more.

   Explain how Felicity might benefit from her daughter being in early years provision. [3]

4. Identify **two** settings that will be suitable for working parents/carers that have a baby. [2]

5. Which of these is a prime area in the EYFS?
   - **A** Mathematics
   - **B** Creative arts and design
   - **C** Physical development
   - **D** Understanding the world [1]

6. Give **two** examples of how early years settings may benefit parents and carers. [2]

7. Sunny Bees is an early years setting. It takes 50 children from six months to five years. It is open throughout the year and also has a breakfast and after-school club. The owner makes a profit from the business.

   Using this information, identify:
   - **a)** the type of provision [1]
   - **b)** the type of early years setting. [1]

8. Give **two** examples of how the facilities of early years settings may vary. [2]

9. A school is very popular with parents. It has admissions criteria. Explain why a school might have admissions criteria. [2]

10. Explain **two** reasons why some parents may choose an early years setting that has a high staff-to-child ratio. [2]

Use your knowledge

Maria and Jordan are looking for an early years setting for their son who is two years old. They are in an area where there is a lot of choice of early years settings. They work from home part-time. They would like their son to have plenty of opportunities to be outdoors. Their son has communication and language difficulties, and they have been told to choose a setting where there are plenty of opportunities for interaction. The family are not sure what type of activities will support their child's development in this area.

Write a presentation that gives information about the different types of early years settings and make recommendations for this family to consider.

Your report should also give information about what the family should consider when they visit different settings.

5 Legislation, policies and procedures in the early years

All those who work in early years must be aware of the laws, policies and procedures (see section 5.2.1 for an explanation of these terms) which are in place around their role. These are very important and you will need to consider them daily when working with children. This chapter looks at these laws, policies and procedures and how they influence what happens in early years settings.

5.1 Regulatory authority

The regulatory authority which exists to monitor standards in education and childcare is Ofsted. This is a government department but has no power to change the law.

Ofsted's main functions or responsibilities are shown in Table 5.1.

Table 5.1 Ofsted's functions and responsibilities

Function	What this means
Inspecting	Carrying out inspections on care settings, education settings, childcare settings, local authorities, adoption and fostering agencies, initial teacher training and teacher development.
Regulating	Creating a set of rules for settings such as early years and children's services, so that their responsibilities are clear and services are suitable.
Reporting	Publishing and reporting on the findings of inspections to settings and parents and enabling policymakers to look at their effectiveness.

> **Regulatory authority** A group which monitors standards in particular professions or organisations, such as health or education.
>
> **Ofsted** Office for Standards in Education, Children's Services and Skills. This is a regulatory authority.

Revision activity

Identify the main functions of Ofsted and write them in your own words.

Typical mistake

Don't think that Ofsted only exists to inspect and report on schools and early years settings – it also inspects, regulates and reports on a range of education and care settings as well as children's services such as adoption and fostering agencies.

5.2 Legislation and frameworks which underpin policy and procedure

Legislation and frameworks influence the way in which all early years settings operate. This is because settings will need to show that they meet legal requirements and that all staff understand what they need to do.

5.2.1 Legislation, framework, policy and procedure definitions

You will need to know the meaning of each of these terms (shown in Table 5.2) as you will come across them regularly in early years settings.

Table 5.2 Definitions of terms

Term	Definition
Legislation	A law or set of laws that have been passed by Parliament.
Framework	A set of standards that must be met.
Policy	An agreed set of actions that have been adopted by an organisation to deal with certain situations.
Procedure	The way in which an organisation carries out a policy.

> **Revision activity**
>
> Make sure you are very clear on the four terms in Table 5.2. Ask someone to test you on their meanings, and give examples of each term.

> **Typical mistake**
>
> Policies and procedures are not the same thing – make sure you know the difference.

5.2.2 Legislation

Legislation affects many aspects of our lives and childcare practice. Figure 5.1 shows a few key pieces of legislation which significantly affect early years settings. These will in turn influence policies and procedures, and the way in which settings are run.

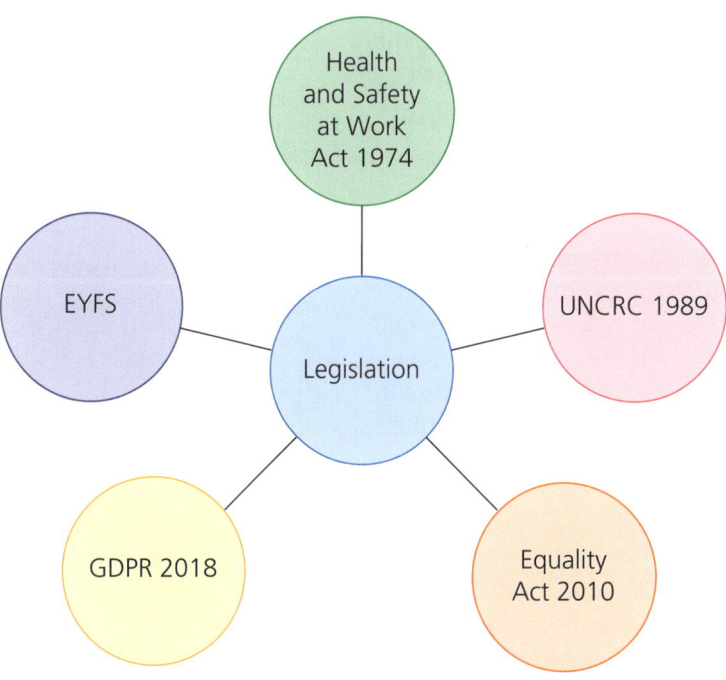

Figure 5.1 Key pieces of legislation for early years settings

> **Exam tip**
>
> When you are learning about a piece of legislation, it is important to remember the year it became law. This is because sometimes legislation is updated later.

Health and Safety at Work etc. Act 1974

The Health and Safety at Work etc. Act 1974 is an important piece of legislation as it sets out what should be done to protect the health, safety and welfare of everyone in the workplace. See also section 5.2.3.

Policy

+ Health and safety: All workplaces are required to have a policy for health and safety to ensure that everyone is kept safe and well. In early years settings, this refers to children, staff and visitors. The policy will set out the roles and responsibilities of the setting and the staff.
+ Food and drink: Settings should have a food and drink policy to ensure that food preparation, hygiene and supervision are carried out safely. The food and drink policy should be read alongside the EYFS statutory framework.
+ Visitors to the setting: The setting's health and safety policy will include information about the importance of monitoring all visitors so that staff and children are kept safe. See also 'Arrival and departure of visitors' under Procedures below.

> **Exam tip**
>
> The key legislation in this section will affect all your work in early years settings. Make sure you learn at least two basic policies and procedures for each piece of legislation.

Figure 5.2 Why is it important for all early years settings to have a food and drink policy?

Procedure

- Risk assessments: These should be carried out regularly in each setting so that potential hazards can be avoided, and action or controls are put in place to stop them from happening. (For more on risk assessments and what is involved, see sections 3.3 and 5.2.3.)
- Safe working practices during food preparation: As well as information in the food and drink policy, there may be a separate section in the setting's health and safety policy. This should set out the importance of hand washing and using personal protective equipment (PPE) when preparing food. (For more on safe working practices during food preparation, see section 5.2.3.)
- Arrival and departure of visitors: All settings should have procedures for signing visitors in and out of the setting. They may also be given badges to wear while they are on the premises. This is to make sure that they can be identified and so that the setting knows who is present in case of emergencies such as a fire. (For more on the arrival and departure of visitors, see section 5.2.3.)
- Reporting accidents: All staff in the setting should know the procedures for reporting accidents. This is a legal requirement under the Reporting of Injuries, Diseases and Dangerous Occurrences Regulations (RIDDOR 2013). Settings will have an accident book so that details of any accidents can be recorded. (For more on reporting accidents and what is involved, see section 5.2.3.)

> **Check your understanding**
>
> 1 Which **two** safe working practices should settings adopt in their procedures around food preparation?

United Nations Convention on the Rights of the Child (UNCRC) 1989

The UNCRC is a comprehensive set of 54 rights or articles for children.

The UNCRC is not in itself legislation. It is an international human rights treaty which affects UK legislation. It was ratified by the UK along with 195 other states, in 1989, as it was the most comprehensive statement on children's rights ever produced. These rights influence early years practitioners' work with children, as they must be respected for each child.

> **Ratified** Formally agreed by government.

> **Revision activity**
>
> Find out which rights protected under the UNCRC are the most relevant to those working in early years.

Check your understanding and progress at www.hoddereducation.co.uk/myrevisionnotes

> **Exam tip**
>
> You will not need to learn every one of the articles in the UNCRC, but it might be useful to learn those which are usually seen as the most important by UNICEF. These are articles 2, 3, 6 and 12; see Table 5.3.
>
> There may also be others which you choose to learn, such as Article 19.

Table 5.3 The general principles of the UNCRC

Article	What it means
Non-discrimination (Article 2)	The Convention applies to every child without discrimination, whatever their ethnicity, sex, religion, language, abilities or any other status, whatever they think or say, and whatever their family background.
Best interests of the child (Article 3)	The best interests of the child must be a top priority in all decisions and actions that affect them.
The right to life, survival and development (Article 6)	Every child has a right to life. Governments must do all they can to ensure that children survive and develop to their full potential.
The right to be heard (Article 12)	Every child has the right to express their views, feelings and wishes in all matters affecting them, and to have their views considered and taken seriously. This right applies at all times, for example during immigration proceedings, housing decisions or the child's day-to-day home life.

Policy

+ Safeguarding: Article 19 of the UNCRC states that all children must be protected from violence, abuse and neglect. It is a legal requirement that all early years settings must have a safeguarding policy, as well as a member of staff who is responsible for keeping children safe. They are usually known as the designated safeguarding lead (DSL). Section 3 of the EYFS statutory framework also sets out requirements for safeguarding in early years settings. (For more on safeguarding procedures, see section 5.2.5.)
+ Play: Article 31 of the UNCRC states that every child has a right to play. Settings are likely to have a play or learning through play policy. This should set out the importance of play and also outline how a range of indoor and outdoor play activities will support children's learning and development.
+ Equality and diversity policy: All settings should have an equality and diversity policy. This has been set out by the UNCRC as well as the Equality Act 2010. (For more on this Act see below, and for procedure see section 5.2.4.)

> **Designated safeguarding lead (DSL)** The person in the setting who is responsible for acting on and monitoring any safeguarding concerns.

Procedure

+ Reporting abuse: In all cases, settings must have agreed procedures for reporting and recording abuse so that staff are clear on what they should do. (For more on reporting abuse, see section 5.2.5.)
+ Providing play: Procedures will set out how the setting provides a range of safe opportunities for indoor and outdoor play, and how early years practitioners can support different play activities.
+ Adapting activities: The UNCRC's principles mean that each child has a right to all activities. This means that, where necessary, activities may need to be adapted so that all children can take part, for example by providing additional equipment or resources.

> **Check your understanding**
>
> 2 a) What does UNCRC stand for?
>   b) Why have its principles been incorporated into law by so many nations?

Equality Act 2010

(See section 5.2.4 for more information on this law.)

The Equality Act was introduced to replace and update nine earlier equality laws in the UK. Under the Act there are nine protected characteristics (shown in Figure 5.3), which you must not discriminate against anyone for having.

> **Discriminate** To treat someone differently based on a characteristic such as race, gender or disability

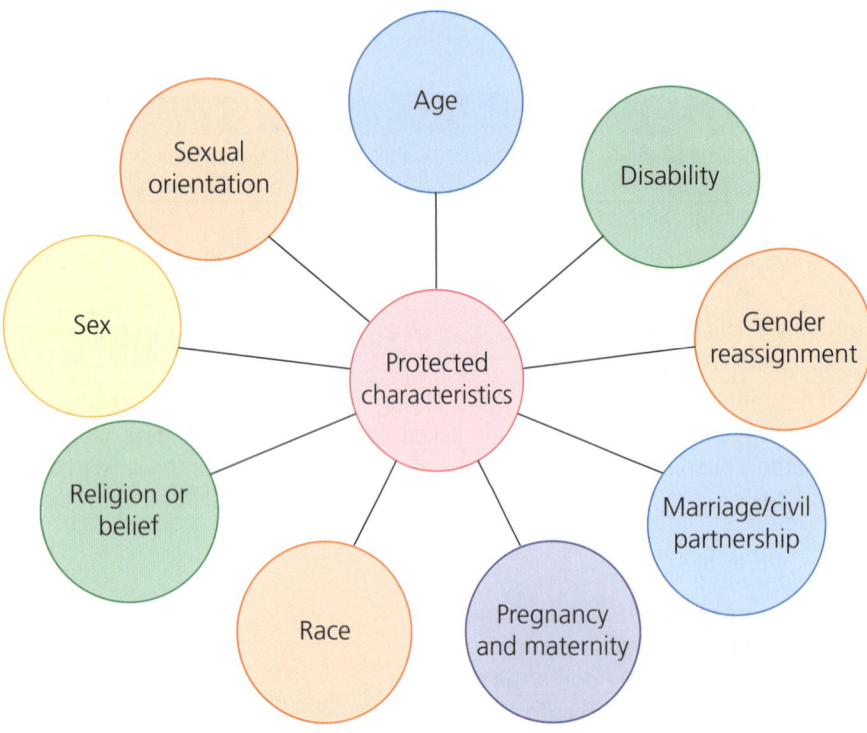

Figure 5.3 Protected characteristics listed in the Equality Act 2010

For example, because pregnancy and maternity is a protected characteristic, this means that someone who is pregnant or has had a child must not be discriminated against by an employer when they apply for a job. This would be illegal under the Equality Act 2010.

Policy

Equality and diversity: All settings are required to have an equality and diversity policy. This will set out the ways in which they are inclusive to all children and staff.

For a more detailed breakdown of these terms and related procedures, see section 5.2.4.

Procedure

- Providing resources that reflect society: All settings should have a range of resources (for example books and toys) that reflect different groups in society. This is important so that each child feels that the setting relates to them.
- Being a good role model: All staff should be positive role models for children through their behaviour and the way in which they talk to others. This is because children copy adults and want to be like them.
- Adjusting activities to ensure everyone can participate: Activities should be open to everyone and may need to be adjusted or changed slightly so that this is possible. For example, providing a ramp and extra space for a wheelchair user.

> **Equality** Individuals are treated in the same way.
>
> **Diversity** The range of values, attitudes, cultures and beliefs held by different people.
>
> **Inclusive** Open to and including everyone.

Check your understanding

3. Name **two** procedures which early years settings should have in place to ensure that they comply with the Equality Act 2010.

Check your understanding and progress at www.hoddereducation.co.uk/myrevisionnotes

Data Protection Act (2018)

The Data Protection Act 2018 (sometimes known as UK GDPR) is legislation about the way in which personal data is used and stored. Settings need to store a range of information about children and staff and this will need to be kept securely. This legislation outlines the principles of how this must be done and people's rights over how their data is used.

Policy

Confidentiality: The early years policy which relates to the Data Protection Act 2018 is the confidentiality or data protection policy. This policy will set out the way in which the setting should store information, who information can be shared with and the length of time it should be kept.

See section 5.2.6 for more information on confidentiality.

Procedure

- Share information with consent: Settings should have procedures in place so that staff are aware when information can be shared with consent, for example whether they can take photographs of children.
- Store information safely: Procedures should be in place for storing information safely, for example in locked cupboards, or password protected if stored on a computer.
- Share information on a 'need to know' basis: Information should only be shared with others where this is necessary, for example if there are any concerns about a child, this should be shared only with the DSL.

> **Revision activity**
>
> Find out about two procedures which early years settings should have in place to ensure that they comply with the Data Protection Act 2018.

EYFS statutory framework

The EYFS statutory framework is a document that sets out standards for the learning, care and development of children in England from birth to five years. It is a statutory document, which means that there is a legal requirement to follow it.

Policy

- Keyworker: Under the EYFS, each child in an early years setting should have their own keyworker (see section 3.1). This means that a member of staff will be responsible for making sure that the child's care meets their individual needs. This also means getting to know them and their families.
- Safeguarding: The EYFS has a section on safeguarding and welfare requirements, which set out the steps that settings will need to take to make sure that children are kept safe. For instance, all staff in the setting will need to have criminal record checks before they can work with children. This is called a DBS (Disclosure and Barring Service) check.
- Health and safety: The EYFS statutory framework also has a section on health and safety. All settings will need to follow health and safety legislation, and ensure that there are clear policies in place that cover this.

> **Check your understanding**
>
> 4 Why must every child in an early years setting be provided with a keyworker?

Procedure

- Ensure an adequate staff–child ratio: There are legal requirements in place which are set out in the EYFS for staff–child ratios. These apply to all early years settings.
- Respond to disclosure: This means that if any staff suspect that a child is at risk for any reason, they must respond by reporting it to the DSL. For more on safeguarding procedures, see section 5.2.5.
- Never use personal mobile phones when working with children: All staff should be aware that personal mobile phones should not be used to take photos when working with children. Photographs should only be taken

using devices which belong to the setting, to ensure that children are protected. Staff should not have personal mobile phones with them while they are in the setting, and these should be locked away in staff areas.

> **Check your understanding**
>
> 5 Which piece of legislation states that settings must have a 'visitors to the setting policy'?

5.2.3 Health and safety procedure

All early years practitioners will be responsible for maintaining health and safety in the setting. This means that they will need to carry out a range of duties and activities regularly to make sure that others are kept safe. Settings will also need to have an allocated responsible person who ensures the health and safety of staff and children.

Responsible person
Someone in the setting who has a particular responsibility, for example health and safety or first aid.

Carry out risk assessments

A risk assessment is the process of finding and acting on any possible hazards which may occur. Risk assessments will need to be regularly carried out when:

+ planning new activities
+ taking children out of the setting
+ setting security, cooking and food safety procedures
+ nappy changing
+ thinking about what to do in case of fire or other evacuation of the setting
+ any one-off events, such as bringing an animal into the setting.

Although it is not possible to remove all risks, the setting will need to show how it takes steps to reduce them, as show in Figure 5.4.

Typical mistake

A written risk assessment is not needed for **all** of the activities in this bullet list, but settings will need to show that they have thought through each scenario and show how they manage risk.

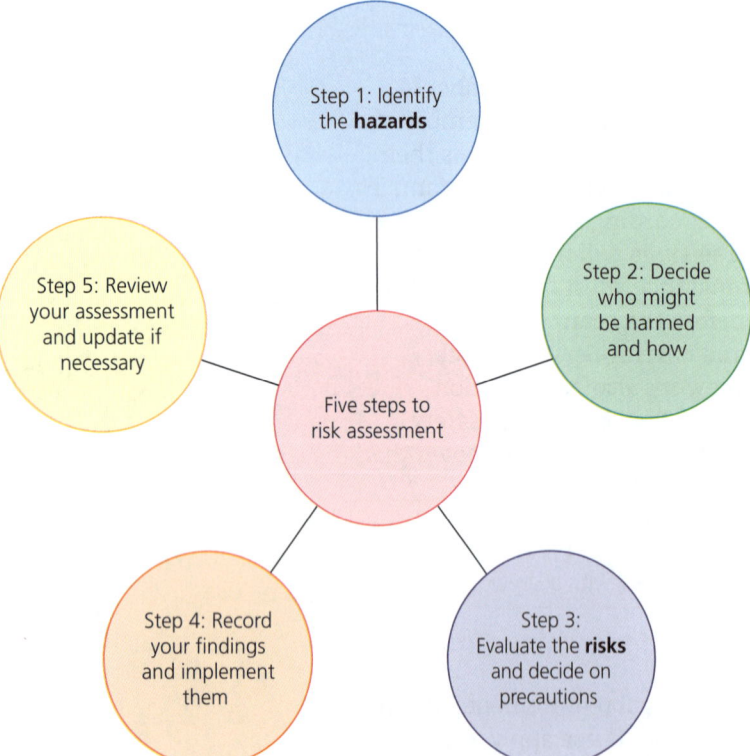

Figure 5.4 The five health and safety steps to risk assessment

There will also need to be other procedures in place to ensure that health and safety is correctly monitored in the setting: see Table 5.4.

Revision activity

+ Write down the five steps to risk assessment.
+ Think of three times when you might need to carry one out.

Check your understanding and progress at www.hoddereducation.co.uk/myrevisionnotes

Table 5.4 The role of the early years practitioner in maintaining health and safety procedures in the setting

Procedure	Role of the early years practitioner
Complete security checks on arrival/departure	<ul><li>All visitors will need to be signed in and out of the setting so that it is clear who is on the premises. Staff are likely to have digital passes, and swipe in and out.</li><li>Settings will need information about who is bringing children to the setting and who will be collecting them. If a different adult will be collecting a child, the setting should be told in advance.</li><li>Staff should not allow children to leave the setting with an adult who has not been authorised by parents or carers.</li></ul>
Make sure equipment is safe to use	<ul><li>All equipment and resources should be checked before use to ensure that they are safe to use.</li><li>Records will need to be kept of checks which have been made to any electrical equipment.</li><li>All equipment must comply with health and safety regulations.</li></ul>
Follow first aid procedures of the setting	<ul><li>The setting will have procedures in place for first aid, including administration of medicines.</li><li>A list of first aiders and the location of first aid boxes should be clear.</li><li>Parents should be informed if a child has received first aid or suffered a head injury.</li></ul>
Follow hand washing, nappy changing and toileting routines	<ul><li>To prevent the spread of infection, staff should ensure that the correct hygiene routines are followed.</li><li>Staff will need to talk to children about this and be good role models, as children might not yet understand the importance of good hygiene habits.</li></ul>
Dispose of bodily fluids and waste safely	<ul><li>Gloves and aprons should always be worn when disposing of bodily fluids and waste.</li><li>General waste and anything which has been used to clean up bodily fluids should be disposed of separately in settings other than childminders or nannies (e.g. nappies, or anything which has been in contact with blood, vomit or urine). These bins will usually be yellow.</li></ul>
Report infectious diseases	<ul><li>Settings must make sure they report any **notifiable diseases** to the local authority so that levels of infection can be monitored.</li></ul>
Report incidents and accidents	<ul><li>Settings must report all **incidents** and **accidents** accurately in an incident or accident book; this is required by EYFS statutory framework and RIDDOR (Reporting of Injuries, Diseases and Dangerous Occurrences Regulations 2013).</li><li>If children are involved, parents and carers must be told immediately. Ofsted must also be told about any serious accident, illness, injury or death of a child.</li></ul>
Follow emergency/evacuation procedures	<ul><li>All settings should have regular emergency and evacuation procedures so that staff and children know what to do in an emergency.</li></ul>
Carry out manual handling safely	<ul><li>There should be a manual handling policy in the setting which has information on correct and safe procedures to be followed when lifting and moving equipment.</li></ul>
Use of PPE	<ul><li>PPE should be used by all staff when needed; e.g. disposable gloves should be worn when changing nappies or cleaning up bodily fluids. These should be provided by the setting.</li></ul>
Ensure food hygiene is maintained	<ul><li>All staff who are preparing and serving food in early years settings should have food hygiene training to prevent food poisoning, which can be dangerous in very young children, and the spread of viruses.</li><li>Food hygiene training includes following safe procedures for washing, preparing, cooking and storing food.</li></ul>
Respond to dietary needs	<ul><li>Parents should be asked about whether their child has any dietary requirements or allergies, so that the right kinds of meals can be provided.</li></ul>
Follow off-site procedures	<ul><li>Although settings do not by law have to complete a written risk assessment when taking children off-site, they must think about how they are managing children's safety and consider how they are managing risks. They must also show that they have considered adult–child ratios. (For more information on ratios, see section 6.3.)</li><li>All vehicles must have appropriate insurance when transporting children.</li></ul>

> **Notifiable disease** A disease which must be reported by law to the authorities. A full list can be found at www.gov.uk/guidance/notifiable-diseases-and-causative-organisms-how-to-report#list-of-notifiable-diseases
>
> **Incident** An event which may cause an injury or develop into an emergency.
>
> **Accident** An unintended incident which may cause physical injury.

5.2.4 Equality and inclusion procedure

All settings should have procedures for equality, diversity and inclusion. Early years practitioners will need to be aware of their responsibilities under these procedures.

Equality

This means that everyone in the setting should be treated fairly and that nobody should be treated less favourably than anyone else. (See section 5.2.2 for the nine protected characteristics under the Equality Act 2010.) To ensure that this takes place, settings will need to:

+ Provide resources that ensure all children can take part in every activity: A range of resources will need to be provided so that all children have an opportunity to take part, whatever their needs.
+ Make reasonable adjustments to activities so that all children have an equal chance to join in: These adjustments may include adapting learning activities (for example enlarging print or pictures for children with a visual impairment, or changing the height of an activity for a child in a wheelchair), providing additional training for staff, or ensuring children with additional needs have the equipment and resources they need.
+ Provide extra explanations so that everyone understands the rules of a game: Children who have communication needs or find it more difficult to understand due to their age may need extra explanations so that they are able to understand.

> **Reasonable adjustments**
> Removing barriers and putting measures in place so that an individual can take part in an activity.

> **Check your understanding**
>
> 6 Give an example of a reasonable adjustment which might need to be made in each case below, to ensure that the child has an equal opportunity to join in with all activities:
>   a) a child with communication needs who relies on specialist equipment
>   b) a child with Type 1 diabetes whose carer administers insulin injections every lunchtime
>   c) a child who has difficulties with hand-eye coordination.

Figure 5.5 Children with additional needs might need extra support to enable them to carry out different activities

Check your understanding and progress at www.hoddereducation.co.uk/myrevisionnotes

Diversity

This means differences in people's values, attitudes, cultures and beliefs. For example, children and adults in the setting might come from a range of religions or cultures.

+ All staff should be able to recognise and celebrate individual differences: This means developing an awareness of individual differences and highlighting what is special about them.
+ Ensure dignity and respect: All children and their parents or carers should be treated with dignity and respect at all times. This means being aware of their wishes and acting on them, as well as making sure that information is kept confidential.
+ Ensure anti-discriminatory practice: No form of discrimination should be tolerated in the setting, and any cases should be reported according to the setting's equality and diversity policy.
+ Provide positive images of all people within society: The setting should provide positive images of different people within society. This may be through displays, books and stories, discussions with children, and off-site visits or visitors to the setting.

> **Anti-discriminatory** Ways of working with children and their families that are inclusive and promote equality and diversity.

Check your understanding

7 Name **three** ways in which early years settings can ensure that diversity is supported and celebrated.

Inclusion

This means that all children in the setting should be given equal access to education and care. We often use the term inclusion when talking about children who have special educational needs and disabilities (SEND).

+ Provide access to appropriate resources and environment: The learning environment and available resources should be suitable and accessible for all children, and reflect a range of needs and backgrounds.
+ Make reasonable adjustments for physical or emotional needs: All children should have their needs met, including those with physical and emotional needs. For example, a child who has difficulty managing their behaviour might need support from an adult if they become distressed.
+ Adapt materials and activities to meet the individual needs of the child and families/carers: Although we have considered the individual needs of the child and how to adapt materials and activities, we might also need to consider the needs of their parents or carers. For example, they might have literacy needs, which means they need support in accessing information from the setting.
+ Provide extra time for activity completion: Some children might need to have extra time to complete activities. For example, a child with communication and language needs might need more time to process information and understand what to do.
+ Follow procedures to support children who speak English as an additional language (EAL): The setting will have a policy for supporting these children, and this will set out the procedures which should be followed. These might include working closely with parents and finding out as much as possible about children's fluency in their home language as well as their level of understanding in English. It will also be helpful for settings to know about parents' level of understanding as they might also need support in developing English language skills.

> **English as an additional language (EAL)** When someone speaks English but it is not their first language.

Check your understanding

8 What is meant by the term 'inclusion' in the context of education and care?

5.2.5 Safeguarding procedure

Safeguarding is an important aspect of your role when working with children. You will need to know about and understand your setting's procedures as it is a responsibility of all staff to keep children safe; these will be found in the setting's safeguarding policy. You will also need to be aware of the safeguarding and welfare requirements in section 3 of the EYFS statutory framework.

> **Safeguarding** The term to use when talking about keeping children safe from abuse or neglect, and protecting them from harm.

Categories and the indicators of abuse

There are four main categories of abuse as explained in Table 5.5 – physical, emotional, sexual and neglect.

Table 5.5 Categories and indicators of abuse

Category of abuse	Meaning	Indicators to look out for
Physical	Deliberately harming a child's body.	+ Physical abuse might take the form of bruising, fractures or burns. Although all children will have physical injuries from time to time, staff should look out for those who have more than others, or who try to cover up any injuries. + Regular absences might also indicate physical abuse.
Emotional	Carrying out abuse such as constant verbal insults, ridiculing or mocking a child. This type of abuse means that a child's emotional development is likely to be affected, and it can be very traumatic for them.	+ Although difficult to identify, emotional abuse can result in a child having low self-esteem, or withdrawing socially from others, including their peers. + Children might also become very quiet, or start to stammer or stutter; these are all signs of anxiety.
Sexual	Inappropriate sexual contact, involvement or behaviour that harms a child.	+ Indicators of sexual abuse might be bruising or pain in genital areas, or the child may show a sudden change in behaviour. + The child might seem uncomfortable or touch their genital area inappropriately or regularly for no reason.
Neglect	Not providing for or meeting a child's basic needs.	+ The child might have untreated illnesses, be regularly hungry or have inappropriate clothing for the weather (e.g. no coat when it is cold). + Neglect might also cause a child to be regularly absent from the setting.

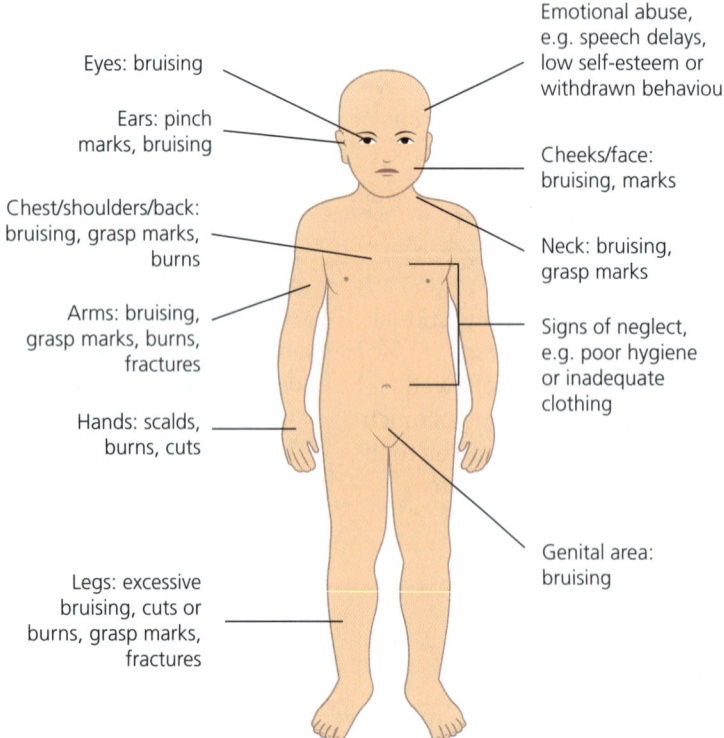

Figure 5.6 All staff need to be aware of the signs of abuse

Check your understanding and progress at www.hoddereducation.co.uk/myrevisionnotes

> **Check your understanding**
>
> 9 Where will you find out about the following:
>   a) procedures for safeguarding in a specific setting
>   b) any additional safeguarding information?

> **Revision activity**
>
> + Divide a piece of paper into four and note down one of the four categories of abuse in each area.
> + Cut up the paper and write the indicators of that form of abuse on the back of the relevant part.
> + Test yourself to see if you can identify the indicators of abuse by looking at the category of abuse on one side of the paper.

Responding to suspected abuse

All staff should be very clear on the procedures for responding to suspected abuse in their setting, as shown in Table 5.6.

Table 5.6 Procedures for responding to suspected abuse in the setting

Responsibility of staff	How to carry out
Observe and record	+ If you have been told about or seen anything which causes you concern, you should write down only what you have seen or been told. + You should only record facts rather than your own judgements. + Keep this information securely in case it is needed later.
Follow guidance, policies and procedures	+ Read your setting's safeguarding policy and follow the procedures for responding to any and all cases of suspected abuse. + Safeguarding the child is a priority.
Put into action **lines of reporting**	+ In all cases, the first line of reporting will be to the DSL. + The DSL will then take responsibility for acting on it and passing the information on. + They will then be the point of contact and know the progress of the case at each stage.
Maintain professional boundaries	+ This means being professional at all times, and making sure all information remains confidential and is only reported to those who need to know. This is important due to the seriousness of the investigation.
Ensure other professionals provide protection	+ By following the correct procedures, safeguarding strategies will automatically be put into place. This means that children will be protected straight away by other professionals.

> **Lines of reporting** The order or direction in which information is passed on.

> **Exam tip**
>
> Make sure you are very clear on safeguarding procedures and what to do in cases of suspected abuse. Safeguarding features regularly in exam questions and is extremely important for your practice, whether or not you are tested on it.

5.2.6 Confidentiality procedure

Maintaining confidentiality is an important part of the role of every early years practitioner. You will need to understand your setting's procedure for confidentiality and why it must be maintained.

> **Confidentiality** The preservation of privileged information concerning children and their families.

Why confidentiality must be maintained

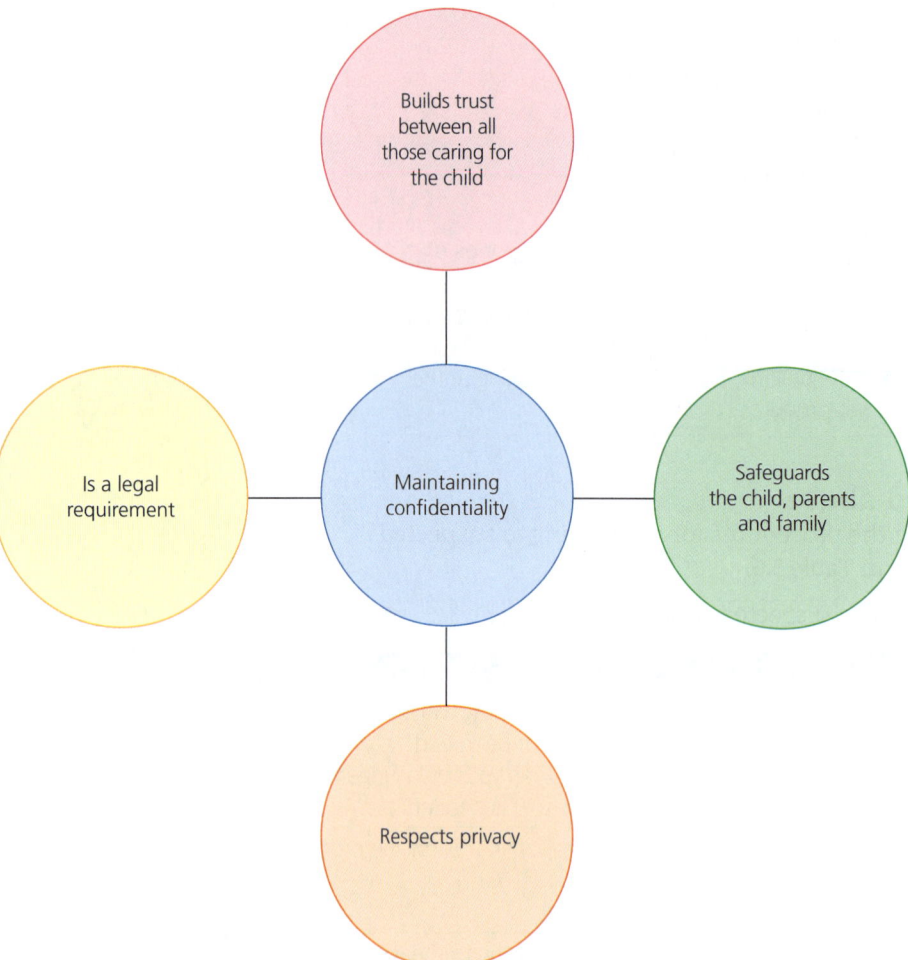

Figure 5.7 Reasons for maintaining confidentiality

You need to remember reasons why confidentiality is important:
+ It builds trust between all those caring for the child: Confidentiality is important for all those who care for the child as it will help them to have positive relationships. It will also help them to develop trust and feel that they can share information freely.
+ Confidentiality safeguards the child, parents and family: Ensuring that information is kept confidential means that the child and their family are protected. Information should only be shared with those who need to know so that they are not put at risk.
+ It is a legal requirement: Under the Data Protection Act 2018 and GDPR, confidentiality is a legal requirement. All staff should be aware that they are required to keep any personal information which they hold about others private.
+ It respects privacy: Settings will sometimes need to be given information about any challenging situations or circumstances at home, for instance, or personal medical issues, so that staff are able to manage the child's needs. Ensuring confidentiality is maintained will ensure that the privacy of children and families is respected.

> **Revision activity**
>
> Create a poster for a staff room which explains why confidentiality must be maintained in the setting and beyond.

Role of the early years practitioner

In early years settings, maintaining confidentiality and following correct procedures will be required in most cases, as shown in Table 5.7.

Table 5.7 Correct procedures for confidentiality

Responsibility of the setting	Procedure
Obtain consent	Parents and carers should give their consent or permission if any information about their child, including photos, is to be seen by others.
Ensure secure handling and storage	Information should be kept securely and handled carefully.
Share information	Information should only be shared with those who need to know.

Protect the child

In some cases, confidentiality might need to be breached, or broken.

This might happen in order to protect the child, if they are put at more risk by maintaining confidentiality (for example, if they are at risk of harm or abuse). In that case it will be necessary to tell the safeguarding lead.

> **Breach** Failure to keep to an agreement.

Whistleblowing

Whistleblowing means that a member of staff is suspected of malpractice by others in the workplace, for example through behaving inappropriately around children. Another member of staff will need to report what has happened to others, usually within but sometimes outside the setting.

Most settings will have a whistleblowing policy, which will set out what should be done in this situation to keep children safe, but also to comply with the law that protects people who whistleblow.

> **Whistleblowing** Reporting malpractice or wrongdoing of someone in your own workplace.
>
> **Malpractice** A failure to carry out professional duties and acting in a way which causes harm.

'Need to know'

Breaching confidentiality, where necessary, should still be according to a 'need to know' principle: it does not mean that suddenly it is fine to tell everyone.

Where there has been malpractice, it may be necessary to share information which is usually confidential so that a person can be brought to justice, for example in court.

Revision activity

Fill in the following table with the meanings of each term:

Term	Meaning
Whistleblowing	
Confidentiality	
To breach confidentiality	
Malpractice	

Exam-style questions

1. Name **two** functions of Ofsted. [2]
2. Which of the following is a set of laws that has been passed by parliament?
   - **A** Committee
   - **B** Legislation
   - **C** Policy
   - **D** Procedure [1]
3. Explain **one** reason why an early years practitioner should ensure food hygiene is maintained. [2]
4. a) Outline three health and safety procedures which early years practitioners should carry out in the setting. [3]
   b) Explain the importance of each one you have chosen. [3]
5. Saanvi is three and attends the setting. Her parents are both from India and her mother has said that for Diwali she would be able to come and talk to the children about how she puts on a sari and to create some Rangoli patterns with them.
   a) Explain why this activity should be encouraged. [1]
   b) Using another example of your choice, describe how involving parents and carers will benefit the setting in other ways. [2]
6. State **two** other ways in which staff can provide positive images of all people within society. [2]
7. Florrie's mother is partially sighted and she recently tripped over twice on the path to the setting when collecting Florrie.

   Discuss what might happen if Florrie's mother were to injure herself badly on the path, and identify ways in which this could be prevented. [6]
8. a) Name **two** things you should do if you suspect abuse. [2]
   b) In each case, explain why you would need to do them. [2]
9. The setting manager keeps personal information on all staff in the office. Which of the following is the most suitable place to store this?
   - **A** A cupboard
   - **B** A filing cabinet
   - **C** A password-protected computer
   - **D** A personal laptop [1]
10. There has been high staff turnover in your setting. You know that one of the assistants in your team has not received induction training, which includes health and safety and safeguarding training.

    Discuss what you would do in this situation, and why it is important for all staff to have this training. [6]

Use your knowledge

Rosie is 13 months old and has been coming to the nursery for a few months. Her mum Sarah is a single parent who has gone back to work full-time. She recently told the setting that she is in a relationship with a new partner.

You have started to notice regular bruising on Rosie and take note of when this is particularly noticeable. She also seems to be regularly distressed and you are concerned, so you go to speak to your DSL.

The DSL thanks you for your concerns. However, she tells you not to be worried as Sarah seems very nice and her partner is female.

Explain and justify what you would do in this situation.

6 Expectations of the early years practitioner

In any job role there will be expectations around behaviour, appearance and professionalism. This means that you need to know what is expected and be familiar with your setting's policies.

6.1 Appearance

REVISED

It is important to remember that your appearance needs to be both professional and practical, and there are several aspects to this. The setting will usually have a dress code that sets out what is required of staff. In some cases, uniforms may need to be worn.

> **Professional** Behaving in a way which shows you are competent and reliable in your job role.

Good personal hygiene

This is important to minimise the spread of infection, give a professional welcoming impression and encourage safe working.

Table 6.1 explains the important aspects of your appearance relating to personal hygiene.

Table 6.1 Personal hygiene aspects of your appearance

Area of body	Requirements for personal hygiene
Hair	Hair should be clean and tied back if long. This is for several reasons: + Long hair can get in the way and be pulled by babies and young children. + Loose hair is unhygienic when preparing food. + Head lice can be spread more easily by head-to-head contact if hair is not tied back.
Nails	Nails should be short and clean. This is for two main reasons: + Dirt can build up under long nails and be difficult to remove easily. Practitioners may be changing nappies and clearing up bodily fluids as well as administering first aid or preparing food so hygiene is very important. + Short nails are more practical when carrying out play activities as nails might catch on children and potentially hurt them. It is also more difficult to carry out some activities with long nails.
Skin	Skin should be clean and fresh smelling. As role models, early years practitioners should show children that they keep themselves clean.

> **Check your understanding**
>
> 1 Give **two** reasons why hair should be clean and tied back if long.

Body art, piercings and tattoos

Table 6.2 explains the important aspects of your appearance relating to body art, piercings and tattoos.

Table 6.2 Appearance aspects related to body art, piercings and tattoos

Area of body	Requirements for body art, piercings and tattoos
Piercings	Piercings should be removed if they could be a safety hazard. For example, babies could pull on hooped or dangly earrings.
Body art and tattoos	Body art and tattoos should be covered if: + they could cause offence in any way + they are unsuitable in content or style for an early years setting.

> **Check your understanding**
>
> 2 Give **one** reason why piercings may not be allowed in a setting.

Clothing and accessories

Clothing and accessories should give a professional welcoming impression, enable early years practitioners to work safely and comfortably and also minimise the spread of infection. See Table 6.3.

Table 6.3 Appearance aspects related to clothing and accessories

Area	Requirements for clothing/accessories
Clean	Clothes should be clean, frequently washed and fresh smelling.
Safe	+ Clothes and accessories should be safe, without tassels, beads, sequins or any other **embellishments**. + These could be hazardous to young children, who might, for example, pull them off and try to put them in their mouths.
Practical	+ Clothing and accessories should be practical and allow for movement. + Clothing should be suitable for both indoor and outdoor wear.
Respectful	+ Clothing and accessories should be respectful to others and there should be no offensive or disrespectful slogans. + Clothing should not be revealing.
In line with policies	Clothing and accessories should meet any uniform requirements and be in line with the setting's policies.

> **Revision activity**
>
> Draw a stick person and use labels to indicate the expectations of an early years practitioner's appearance.

> **Embellishment** A decoration which has been added to something.

Figure 6.1 Comfortable clothes are important when working with young children

> **Exam tip**
>
> To help you remember the three areas covered in section 6.1, try **HBC**: **H**ygiene, **B**ody art, **C**lothing.

6.2 Behaviour

REVISED

As an early years practitioner, you should be aware of the impact of your behaviour on others, particularly as you will be working with young children who will notice what you say and do.

Work within the policies and procedures of the setting to meet legislation

You should follow behaviour requirements as presented in your setting's policies and procedures. See Table 6.4 for these points.

Table 6.4 How your behaviour matches the expectation of the setting and meets legislation

Expectation of the setting	What this means
Carry out health, safety and hygiene practices	+ Health and safety will be included at induction and all staff should be familiar with the setting's policy (see page 61). + All settings will have policies and procedures around health, safety and hygiene so that they can meet the requirements of the Health and Safety at Work etc. Act 1974. + A member of staff will be responsible for monitoring health and safety but all staff are responsible for keeping children safe. + Settings will need to carry out risk assessments to identify and prevent risks. + Routines will include regular cleaning, safety checks, food hygiene procedures and fire drills.

Check your understanding and progress at www.hoddereducation.co.uk/myrevisionnotes

Table 6.4 Continued

Expectation of the setting	What this means
Show respect	+ Early years practitioners should be professional, and show respect and consideration to parents and carers. + The dignity of children and parents or carers should always be maintained. + Confidentiality should always be observed in line with data protection legislation.
Dress code	+ All staff should be aware of and follow the setting's dress code (see also section 6.1).

> **Typical mistake**
> Don't think that health and safety is the responsibility of someone else – all staff are responsible for ensuring that the setting is safe.

Maintain professional boundaries

This means ensuring that your behaviour is appropriate for a professional environment.

+ **Appropriate relationships:** In an early years setting you will have responsibilities towards children, parents and colleagues. Relationships with them should not be personal because it is more important to be focused on your role. It is also important to avoid showing any favouritism towards children and parents, and to avoid any accusations of inappropriate relationships.
+ **Maintain confidentiality:** You should always remember confidentiality and keep information private in line with your setting's confidentiality policy (for more on confidentiality see section 5.2.6).
+ **Use of mobile phone:** Settings will ask staff to keep personal mobile phones locked away during the day for safeguarding reasons. The setting will usually own phones and cameras which staff can use when they are on trips.
+ **Use of social media:** Social media should not be used in the setting, and although you can use it outside the setting you should be careful of making 'friends' or connections which do not allow you to keep professional boundaries (see page 65 in Chapter 5).

> **Revision activity**
> Go back to section 5.2.6 and revise some of the reasons why confidentiality must be maintained in the setting.

> **Revision activity**
> Create a leaflet for volunteers and students in your setting, outlining the requirements for professionalism while they are on placement.

Positive attitude

Having a positive attitude means having personal qualities which will benefit others as well as yourself. Figure 6.2 shows the characteristics needed for a positive attitude.

> **Personal qualities** An individual's characteristics and personality traits.

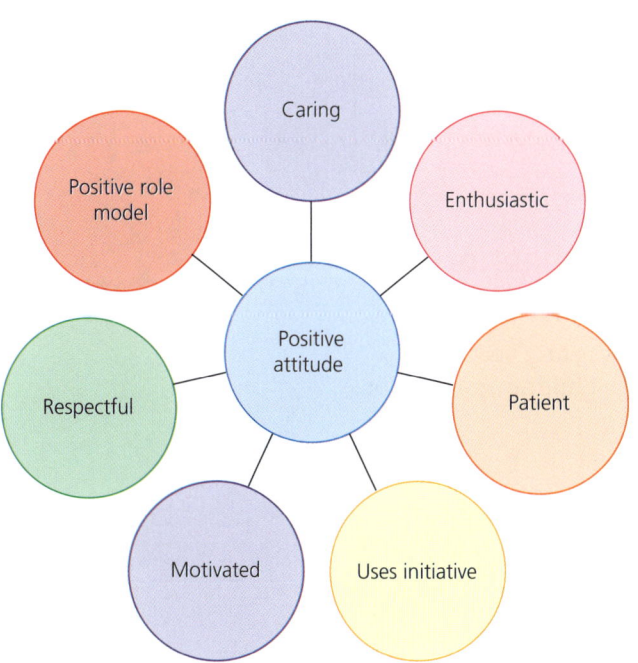

Figure 6.2 Personal qualities required for a positive attitude

- **Caring:** Noticing things that matter to others and taking time to talk to them.
- **Enthusiastic:** Being cheerful and enthusiastic about what you are doing will help others to do the same.
- **Patient:** This is an essential part of your work as an early years practitioner. Children need adults to help them work through their thoughts and feelings. You will also need to be flexible and allow more time to children if they need it.
- **Uses initiative:** This means seeing what needs to be done and doing it, without needing to be told by someone else.
- **Motivated:** Keep being interested in your career and in developing your role, and be inspired by what you do.
- **Respectful:** Treat people in a way which values them. Avoid making judgements or assumptions about them.
- **Positive role model:** A positive role model is someone who shows others through their behaviour that they are helpful and considerate.

> **Exam tip**
>
> To help you remember some of the personal qualities needed by early years practitioners, think about ways in which you might show a colleague that you are caring for them and making the best impression you can.

Figure 6.3 Use your initiative when carrying out duties in the setting

> **Revision activity**
>
> Create a person specification for someone who works in early years which sets out the kinds of personal qualities which are needed when applying for jobs in the role.

> **Check your understanding**
>
> 3 List **four** ways in which early years practitioners can show others that they have a positive attitude.

Effective verbal and non-verbal communication with the child, parent, carer or team members

Communication is a very important part of your role as an early years practitioner, as it will help you to form relationships with children, parents or carers and other staff.

Verbal communication

Reflect the child's age and stage of development

Remember to think carefully when communicating with young children, and remember to allow for their age and stage of development.

At the very earliest stages of learning language, children will still be building up their vocabulary and you will need to use facial expressions, body language and gestures alongside spoken language.

Check your understanding and progress at www.hoddereducation.co.uk/myrevisionnotes

Promote the child's learning and development

When speaking to children, remember to point out words and meanings that may be unfamiliar to them so that you can promote their learning and development. By helping children learn to verbalise their thoughts, you will be giving them the tools to put their ideas and feelings into words.

You should spend time talking to children as much as you can, because verbal communication will support their thinking skills as well as their language.

Figure 6.4 How is this early years practitioner showing that they are communicating effectively with the child?

Use clear language

Always use clear language with young children when speaking to them. Speak slowly and try to use vocabulary that you know they will understand. Take into account any additional needs such as hearing impairments.

If parents or carers speak EAL, you may need to check their understanding if you are passing on important information.

Appropriate for the situation

You should think about the situation when communicating with others. For example, in a meeting with parents or colleagues you might need to use more formal language.

> **Check your understanding**
>
> 4 List **four** ways in which you can show effective verbal communication with others.

Non-verbal communication

We all use non-verbal communication, sometimes without realising we are doing it. Non-verbal communication means passing information to others without using speech.

+ **Active listening** means giving people your full attention when they are talking to you. This includes:
  + looking directly at others when they are talking to you, and in the case of young children, getting down to their level to make eye contact
  + using facial expressions and showing that you are listening
  + acknowledging what others are saying by nodding and using gestures as well as responding verbally.

> **Active listening** Giving people your full attention and listening to them carefully.

- Sensitive and respectful: This means being aware of others' situation or feelings when talking to them; for example, being considerate if they are feeling unwell or if they are unable to listen at a particular time because they are busy.
- Body language can take different forms. As well as showing how interested you are in what others are saying, it can also include appropriate touch, mannerisms and facial expressions. You should be aware of your body language as well as that of other people, and remember that it may be negative as well as positive.

> **Typical mistake**
>
> Don't think that communication is only verbal and can only be made through speech – remember about non-verbal communication, such as making eye contact, smiling and nodding.

> **Revision activity**
>
> Write a sentence about each of the following to explain what they mean:
> - professional boundaries
> - being a positive role model
> - active listening
> - dress code
> - body language.

6.3 Attendance and punctuality

REVISED

As a member of staff, it is important that the setting can trust you to be there on time each day and know that you are dependable. This is part of your professional role in any job, as you will need to build confidence with your colleagues.

You should also remember that as a volunteer or student, attendance and punctuality are important for the same reasons: the setting expects you to be there and will be relying on you.

Attendance

Attendance is important for four reasons:
- Ensures that adult–child ratios are met: The EYFS statutory framework sets out specific age-related adult–child ratios for early years settings. If early years practitioners do not come to work, these ratios will be affected which may mean that there are not enough staff members.
- Children are safe: Having the correct number of adults in the setting will mean that children are supervised safely. As very young children are not aware of any dangers, they need to be watched all of the time.
- Parents and carers can rely on the early years setting to care for their child: The setting is put in a position of trust by parents and carers, and they need to know that their child is being cared for effectively.
- Children's needs can be met: There should be enough adults in the setting to meet the needs of individual children. This is to ensure that they have access to food and drink, sleep and rest, and that their learning and development needs are being met. For children who have SEND or for those with medical needs, more adults may need to be available. (For more on special educational needs, see Chapter 7.)

> **Adult–child ratio** How many staff there are to children. For example, a ratio of 1:3 would mean that there is one adult member of staff to every three children.
>
> **SEND** Special educational needs and disabilities.

> **Exam tip**
>
> You are not likely to be asked the specific age-related adult–child ratios in the EYFS for your exams, but you should know where to find this information in the EYFS statutory framework if necessary.

> **Check your understanding**
>
> 5 Why is it important that adult–child ratios are met in the setting?

Check your understanding and progress at www.hoddereducation.co.uk/myrevisionnotes

Ways to deal with attendance issues

Table 6.5 explains why attendance issues are important.

Table 6.5 The impact on the setting of staff attendance

What to do	Why this is important
Inform manager if you are unable to attend the setting due to illness.	This will allow your manager to find another member of staff to cover for you.
Ensure that personal appointments are booked outside work time.	This might not always be possible, but it is important to try to keep personal appointments in work time to a minimum so that there are enough staff members.
Show reliability by keeping to agreed work patterns.	Make sure you double-check any shift patterns so that you can be relied upon to be at work at the right time.

> **Check your understanding**
>
> 6 Rowan has an important medical appointment for the following week during work hours. He has been waiting for the appointment for a few weeks and feels that he should go to it. Would it be acceptable for Rowan to go to the appointment, or should he try to change it?

Timekeeping

Good timekeeping is essential for the smooth running of the setting.

- Ensures that the early years setting can open safely: When staff are punctual, it means that managers can rely on them to arrive on time so that they can plan safely.
- Activities are ready for the children when they arrive: When staff arrive on time, it gives them plenty of time to set up activities and resources for children and check that they are safe.
- Effective teamwork can take place: By arriving on time, staff show that they can rely on one another and not put pressure on their colleagues. This will have an impact on morale in the setting as it will mean that the team will run more efficiently.
- Children are well cared for, and their needs are met: When staff are on time and are reliable, the needs of children are more likely to be met. This is because everyone will be well prepared.

> **Check your understanding**
>
> 7 Give **two** reasons why timekeeping is important.

Ways to maintain expected timekeeping

Whether you are a volunteer or a member of staff, you should always be on time, as others will be relying on you to be there. You will need to:
- arrive on time at the start of the day
- return on time after a break
- finish at the agreed time at the end of the day.

> **Revision activity**
>
> Create an information sheet for new members of staff which includes expectations for timekeeping and attendance.

Exam-style questions

1. An early years worker who is a smoker has gone out at lunchtime to have a cigarette.

   Give **one** reason why the early years worker has not met expected requirements when they return back into the setting. [1]

2. An early years practitioner has a tattoo on their forearm. The weather is very warm and they have worn a short-sleeved top to work. The early years employer has sent the practitioner home to change their clothing and cover their arms.

   Explain why this may have happened. [2]

3. Give **two** reasons why an early years practitioner should wear practical clothing. [2]

4. What do 'professional boundaries' mean in a childcare/early years setting?
   - A Being at work on time
   - B Behaving professionally in a work environment
   - C Keeping all your professional equipment at work
   - D Making sure that the boundaries of the setting, such as fences and walls, are kept in good repair [1]

5. Give **three** examples of what is meant by being professional as an early years practitioner. [3]

6. Name **two** health, safety and hygiene practices which will need to be carried out in the setting to meet health and safety legislation. [2]

7. Ellie works in a nursery. Although her daughter Rebecca left several years ago, she knows many of the parents who have children enrolled there as they met when their children spent time at the nursery together. Several of them have invited her to join a group chat on a social networking app so that they can keep in regular touch about their children.

   Write a paragraph discussing what Ellie should do in this situation and why. How should she respond to the other parents if they repeatedly ask her to join? [6]

8. Which **one** of these is an example of having a positive attitude?
   - A Arriving late for work
   - B Taking a long time for breaks
   - C Using initiative
   - D Talking to parents on social media [1]

9. Outline, with examples, why clear verbal communication is important in the early years setting:
   a) with colleagues [3]
   b) with children. [3]

10. Give **one** reason why the employer at an early years setting should be informed as soon as possible if an adult (employee) cannot come to work. [1]

Use your knowledge

Tejal has started a new role in a nursery setting. As part of her induction, she has been given a handbook and told that there are expectations for staff which she must observe when she is at work.

Create a poster outlining these staff expectations which could be displayed within the setting to reinforce the requirements for the people that work there.

Within the poster information, explain why it is important that staff are familiar with the handbook and that they should follow the setting's expectations. Include examples of the impact that putting in place the guidelines (or the results of not doing so) will have on the children in the setting.

Check your understanding and progress at www.hoddereducation.co.uk/myrevisionnotes

7 Roles and responsibilities within early years settings

This chapter looks at the different roles and responsibilities of those who work in early years settings, as well as professionals outside the setting that you may have contact with. As an early years practitioner, you will need to know how to work in partnership with others so that you can support children in the setting more effectively.

7.1 Early years practitioner roles

REVISED

You will need to know about and understand the general roles of those who work in early years settings.

Roles

Figure 7.1 outlines the different roles of those who work in early years settings.

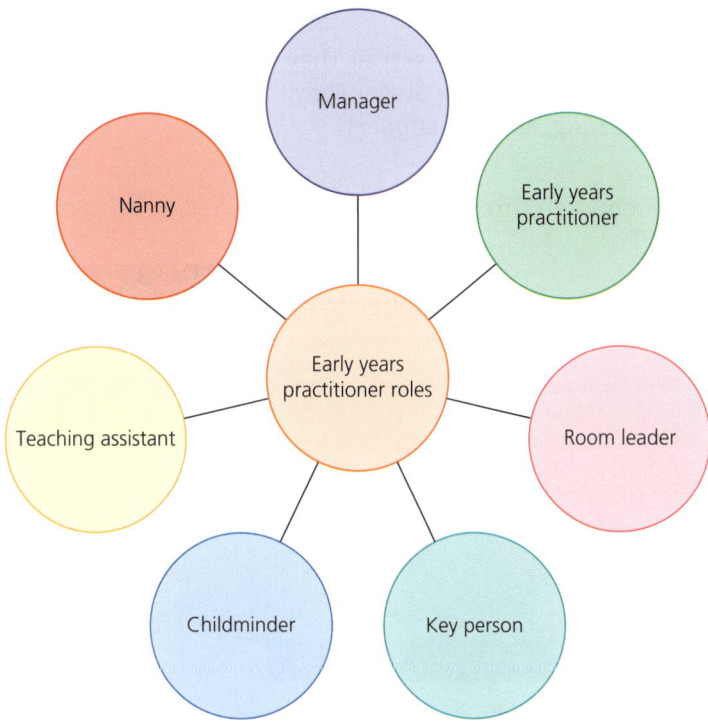

Figure 7.1 Early years practitioner roles

Manager (or person in charge of the setting)
This person is responsible for the care and development of the children in the setting as well as making sure families are supported where needed.

The manager is in charge of staffing, budgets, health and safety, and setting policies and procedures. They are also usually the DSL.

Early years practitioner
The EYP is a designated role within early years, which will mean the practitioner has a Level 2 qualification in early years care and education.

Their role includes:
+ working with parents and carers
+ liaising with other professionals

+ meeting children's care and development needs
+ observing and planning
+ developing effective interactions with children.

Room leader
A room leader is an experienced practitioner, qualified at Level 3, who is responsible for running a room in a setting.

Key person
This is a member of staff in an early years setting who works with a designated child and their family and gets to know them and their specific needs. A key person will have other responsibilities in the setting; for example they could also be a room leader or EYP.

> **Revision activity**
>
> Research the role of the key person in an early years setting.

Childminder
A childminder looks after other people's children in their own home. They will need to plan and provide a variety of provision to support the children's learning and development along with holistic care (see Chapter 1).

Teaching assistant
A teaching assistant works in a school, and so in an early years setting they will be in reception and nursery classes within the Foundation Stage. They work with teachers to support teaching and learning, and will support individual children as well as small groups.

Teaching assistants will also work with older children throughout the school.

Nanny
A nanny usually lives with a family and looks after a child or children to meet their needs in their home.

> **Check your understanding**
>
> 1 Outline **three** aspects of the role of a manager of an early years setting.

> **Typical mistake**
>
> Don't confuse the role of a childminder and a nanny. The N in nanny might help you remember: '**N**ot in the practitioner's home'.

> **Revision activity**
>
> Complete the following table:
>
> | Position | Role |
> |---|---|
> | Nanny | |
> | Childminder | |
> | Early years practitioner | |
> | Room leader | |

Responsibilities
As well as having their specific roles, all staff in early years settings will share a number of responsibilities.

To keep children safe

Table 7.1 explains the staff's responsibility in keeping children safe.

Table 7.1 Responsibilities to keep children safe

Responsibility	What this involves
Prepare and maintain a safe environment	Making sure that the setting is safe for children at all times and looking out for hazards in the environment.
Complete risk assessments	Being aware of the likelihood of risk and, where needed, complete a formal risk assessment, for example when taking children out of the setting. (For more on risk assessments see section 5.2.3.)
Work in partnership with others	Being able to work as part of a team with colleagues both within and outside the setting to keep children safe and well. (For more on partnership working, see section 7.2.)
Provide supervision of children	All children in the setting will need to be supervised at all times and in line with the age-related adult–child ratios in the EYFS statutory framework.
Follow policies	Everyone in the setting must be aware of and follow policies around safety issues, such as the health and safety, online safety and safeguarding policies.

> **Check your understanding**
>
> 2 Name **two** policies which all staff will need to follow in order to keep children safe in early years settings.

Support healthy development

All staff are responsible for supporting and promoting children's healthy development, which can be done in different ways while they are in the setting.

Figure 7.2 Why is this an example of a healthy snack?

- Staff must provide access to healthy snacks, including drinking water at mealtimes: They should always talk to children about why healthy snacks and water are important. They should also have regular routines in place for snacks and mealtimes.
- They must support children's wellbeing: Early years workers should be aware of their role in supporting children's wellbeing. Children should feel able to talk through their thoughts and feelings or any worries and should be supported by adults in doing this, as it will help to support their social and emotional development.

Settings will also have a designated safeguarding lead (DSL) so that staff can raise any concerns about a child with them.

- Opportunities for exercise: Practitioners should make sure they talk to children while they are in the setting about why exercise is important, and create opportunities for them to exercise, both indoors and outdoors.
- Planning and supporting transitions: All children need and benefit from routines, and transitions mean a change. Children's wellbeing is supported by having information about transitions in advance so that they can ask questions about what is going to happen. Staff should plan for expected transitions which may occur, such as moving on to another setting (such as school) or managing a change in staff at the setting. (For more on transitions, see section 2.4).
- Implement hygiene and health routines: This means putting routines into place around hand washing after toileting and nappy changing, as well as keeping food preparation areas clean, and talking to children about why these are important. (For more on hygiene and health routines, see section 3.2.1.)

> **Exam tip**
>
> Make sure you know the difference between expected and unexpected transitions.

> **Check your understanding**
>
> 3 Name **three** ways in which early years practitioners can support the healthy development of children in the setting.

Promote development

There are a number of important approaches to promoting children's development:
- Plan development opportunities and activities: All early years staff are responsible for planning activities which promote children's development in line with the EYFS statutory framework. (For more on planning activities, see section 3.2.2 and Chapter 9.)
- Talk to children during play, activities and routines: Talking to young children is an important part of supporting their development. You can ask them questions about what is happening, as well as give them information and new vocabulary as they are working on activities to support their language and develop their ideas.

Communication and language skills also play a key part in supporting children's cognitive development. (For more on areas of development and how they are interconnected, see Chapter 1.)
- Offer ideas and encouragement: By talking to the child and offering encouragement during activities, you will help to support their perseverance and resilience, which are important aspects of their development.
- Create an enabling environment: All early years practitioners are responsible for creating enabling environments. This means making sure that both indoor and outdoor learning environments are stimulating and inclusive for all children.
- Observe and assess children's learning: Practitioners observe children in different ways when they are carrying out learning activities as this helps to assess their learning and plan future activities. Observations and assessments may be formative or summative. (For more on observations, see Chapter 8.)
- Plan activities and routines based on children's needs: All children's needs should be met by the activities and routines in the setting, particularly those of any children who have SEND.
- Adapt activities, resources and the environment: You might need to adapt activities, resources or the environment to meet the specific needs of children and ensure that they are able to access them.

Enabling environment An environment that supports children's learning and independence

Check your understanding and progress at www.hoddereducation.co.uk/myrevisionnotes

Figure 7.3 How can you make sure that environments are stimulating and inclusive for all children?

> **Exam tip**
>
> To help you remember the difference between formative and summative assessment, summative assessment is a summary of the child's progress at the end of a period of time.

Work in partnership

All early years professionals will need to be able to work with others to ensure that the needs of the children are met: see Table 7.2. (For more on this, see section 7.2.)

Table 7.2 A summary of how to work in partnership

Partnership with …	How to achieve this
Parents/carers	Have an **open door policy** and make sure that communication between the setting and parents is always a priority.
External professionals	Make sure that external professionals are given the information which is needed in order to support the needs of the child. (For more on roles outside early years settings, see section 7.4.)
Participate in teamwork	Build up good relationships and communication with colleagues, so that any areas of conflict are managed effectively. (For more on partnership working, see section 7.2.)

Open door policy People are always welcome to talk to the setting about any questions or concerns whenever they have them, without waiting to be invited to comment.

External professional A professional working with children and families who is not based in a setting

> **Revision activity**
>
> Write a presentation for students considering a career in early years, to outline the different roles and responsibilities of those working in early years settings.

7.2 Partnership working in the early years

REVISED

You will need to know about and understand what is meant by 'partnership working'. This term means the different services and professionals working together with other teams or people to meet the child's and/or family's needs.

7.2.1 How partnership working benefits the child, family and early years practitioner

To understand partnership working, we need to look at how it benefits each person involved.

The child

Figure 7.4 summarises the benefits to the child of partnership working, explained in more detail below.

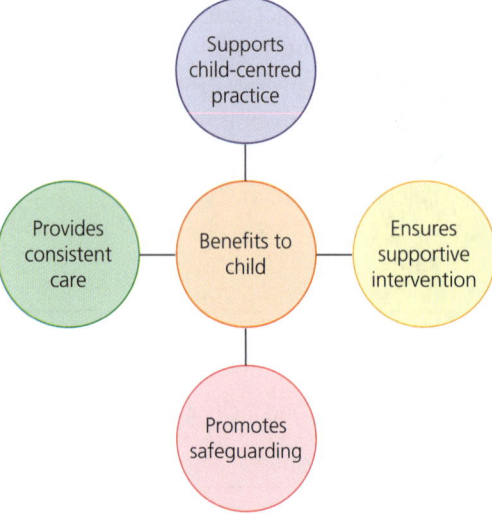

Figure 7.4 Benefits of partnership working for the child

+ Partnership working supports **child-centred practice** that meets children's holistic needs. When professionals work together, the child and their needs should be at the centre of their work. All those who work with the child should ensure that they do all they can to pass information on to others when needed.
+ It ensures that supportive **intervention** is made when a child is not meeting age-expected milestones. If any professional feels that a child is not meeting age-expected milestones, they should make others working with the child aware of this so that appropriate intervention can be put in place.
+ It promotes safeguarding to ensure that children are protected from harm. Safeguarding concerns should always be shared immediately and directly with the DSL, so that they can be referred on appropriately, for example to social services.
+ It provides consistent care, giving emotional and physical security. Young children need to have consistency and routines to feel that they are supported effectively. Partnership working will help them to feel supported and reassured, and to know that they will always be cared for, both physically and emotionally.

> **Child-centred pactice** Decisions are based on the needs and interests of the child
>
> **Intervention** In an education context, an intervention is usually a short series of activities designed to support a child's needs.

Check your understanding

4 Outline **three** ways in which partnership working benefits the child.

The family

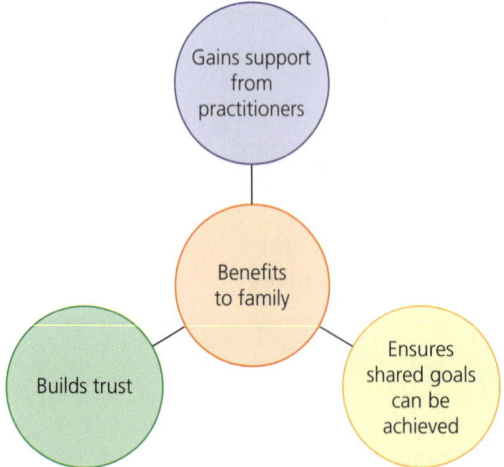

Figure 7.5 Benefits of partnership working for the family

Check your understanding and progress at www.hoddereducation.co.uk/myrevisionnotes

Figure 7.5 summarises the benefits to the family of partnership working, explained in more detail below.

+ Gaining support from practitioners with a different perspective or experience: Families will benefit from talking to early years practitioners who might have a different experience or perspective from their own.

   Practitioners may be able to help them with strategies to meet their child's needs and provide them with new contacts or organisations to support them where needed.

+ Partnership working ensures that shared goals can be achieved and everyone is united in their approach: All those who have contact with specific children should be working towards the same goals. Working with practitioners will help families to support the child and their needs more effectively.

+ It builds trust so that information can be shared to support the child: Good partnership working will mean that all those working with the child are able to build trust with parents and families. This will mean that information is more likely to be shared for the benefit of the child.

Figure 7.6 How do families benefit from partnership working?

Early years practitioner

Figure 7.7 summarises the benefits to the early years practitioner of partnership working, explained in more detail on the next page.

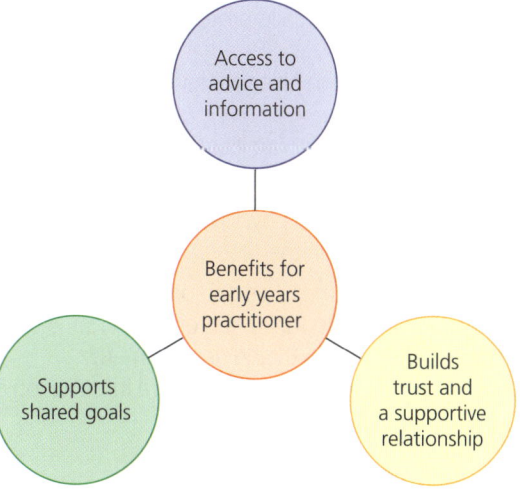

Figure 7.7 Benefits of partnership working for the early years practitioner

- Through partnership working, practitioners will have access to advice and information which will inform planning of activities and routines to promote children's development. Partnership working will help to ensure that early years practitioners have as much information as they can about the children in their care. This will ensure that they are in the best position to support children's learning and development in the setting.
- Partnership working builds trust and creates a supportive relationship where information can be shared. Where practitioners have regular contact with others, a more trusting and supportive relationship will be formed and information is more likely to be shared effectively.
- It supports shared goals and everyone can work to their strengths and support each other: Regular contact will mean that professionals are able to work more closely on shared goals with early years practitioners and support one another more effectively.

> **Revision activity**
>
> Cover the text above or copy and complete the table below to show how partnership working benefits the child, family and early years practitioner.
>
> | Role | Benefits of partnership working |
> |---|---|
> | Child | |
> | Family | |
> | Early years practitioner | |
>
> Check your answers against this book. What did you miss?

7.3 Specialist roles within early years settings

REVISED

Within the setting there will be some specialist roles which some staff will be responsible for in addition to their general role and responsibilities. In the case of childminders, these will all be part of their role unless they employ additional staff.

Table 7.3 Specialist roles within settings

Role	Responsibilities
Special educational needs and disabilities co-ordinator (SENDCo)	This person: + co-ordinates provision for children with special educational needs and disabilities + works with other staff to ensure that the needs of the children are met within the setting + is responsible for overseeing, assessing, planning and monitoring the progress of children with SEND.
Designated Safeguarding Lead (DSL)	This is the named person responsible for child protection for children in the setting. They will: + ensure policies and procedures are in place for safeguarding children + make referrals to external agencies + monitor the needs of children and their families/carers.
Physical activity and nutrition co-ordinator (PANCo)	The PANCo: + acts as a champion for best practice in physical activity and nutrition + promotes health and wellbeing within the setting.
Key person for each child (a requirement of the EYFS)	The key person is a vital role in the setting. This person: + gets to know families and works with their children + offers care to promote children's growth and development + liaises with families to develop relationships and share information about children.

Check your understanding and progress at www.hoddereducation.co.uk/myrevisionnotes

> **Check your understanding**
>
> 5 What do these stand for?
>   a) SENDCo
>   b) PANCo
>   c) DSL
>   d) EYFS

7.4 Specialist roles outside early years settings

REVISED

Professionals from outside the setting might also be asked to come in to support the early years team in different ways.

SEND teams

The SENDCo might call on a range of external professionals to help and advise the team when supporting children's needs. For the purpose of this qualification, you need to know about the roles of physiotherapists and educational psychologists.

+ Physiotherapist: A physiotherapist helps with movement and exercise. This might be needed where a child has a disability, illness or injury and needs to develop their muscle strength.
+ Educational psychologist: An educational psychologist may be asked to come into the setting to assess a child in cases where early years staff have concerns about their learning and development.

Both of these professionals may also be involved if a child already has an EHCP (Education, Health and Care Plan) and provide advice about how the setting can support the child.

> **EHCP (Education, Health and Care Plan)** A document which outlines the care and support a child or young person will need in order to meet their potential up to the age of 25.

Figure 7.8 How does a PANCo influence children's diets within the setting?

Health professionals

Children might need attention from the following health professionals:

+ General practitioner (GP): A GP is a doctor who diagnoses and treats medical conditions. In some cases a GP will refer a baby or child to other professionals if they have concerns about their development.
+ Paediatrician: This is a doctor who has had additional training and specialises in the treatment and care of babies, children and young people.
+ Health visitor: A health visitor works with children and families to support and promote health and development in babies and children up to five years. A health visitor is usually a nurse or midwife who has had additional training and can advise on a range of childhood illnesses as well as children's care and development.

> **Check your understanding**
>
> 6 Choose a health professional and state why they may need to work with early years professionals.

Children's social care

A social worker and family support worker can assist children and families.

Social worker

A social worker provides assessment of a child and their family's needs, and offers a range of support to ensure a child is protected and well cared for. They work with children who are at risk of abuse and neglect, and support foster carers where needed.

A social worker will also refer families to other agencies if needed for additional support.

> **Typical mistake**
>
> Social workers do not only work with children and families; they might also work with other groups such as elderly people, young offenders, refugees and asylum seekers, and those with learning and physical disabilities.

Family support worker

Families might be referred for family support by social workers when they need additional help.

A family support worker provides practical advice and support to individuals and families in need on a range of issues. Their role is to help parents and families through particular issues, such as debt management, homelessness, mental health issues, or drug and alcohol addiction.

> **Check your understanding**
>
> 7 What is the difference between a social worker and a family support worker?

> **Exam-style questions**
>
> 1 In which role does the early years practitioner look after children in the practitioner's own home?
>   A Childminder
>   B Teaching assistant
>   C Room leader
>   D Nanny [1]
>
> 2 Give **two** responsibilities of all those who work in an early years setting. [2]
>
> 3 A nurse is coming into your setting to talk to the children about how to keep healthy and why this is important. You have been asked to sit with groups of children and prepare some questions to ask her.
>   Explain why activities like this are important, and discuss why they are part of the responsibilities of early years practitioners. [3]
>
> 4 A teaching assistant supports the learning and development of young children.
>   What kind of setting is this person working in?
>   A A nursery
>   B A school
>   C A childminder's setting
>   D A crèche [1]
>
> 5 Sammi is working alongside Emma, who is a room leader. Sammi has some concerns about the wellbeing of one of the children in the room. Explain what Sammi's response should be. [2]
>
> 6 Roz is a single parent with four-year-old twins, who attend a childminder's setting. Marley and Dan both have communication and language needs, and have been working with a speech and language therapist. They have targets to work on with Roz. The childminder has asked for a partnership meeting to discuss the twins' needs.
>   a) Who should be invited to the meeting? [2]
>   b) Explain the importance of partnership working in this situation. [2]
>
> 7 Outline what an early years practitioner should do first if they have concerns about a child's learning and development. [1]
>
> 8 What is partnership working? [2]
>
> 9 State **two** aspects of the role of a key person. [2]
>
> 10 Bonnie is in foster care, and her foster parents bring her to the setting. Which specialist professional might be involved with her care and wellbeing? [1]

> **Use your knowledge**
>
> Mile is almost four years old. She started at the setting six months ago and is now living with foster parents, and you are her keyworker. Up until then, she had a disrupted and traumatic home life, and now she does not have any contact with her birth family.
>
> Mile has speech and language delay which means that she has difficulty understanding language as well as putting into words what she wants to say. Both you and other childcare staff have also said that she is reluctant to communicate with other children and prefers to play on her own. You have started to make some picture cards for her to help her to indicate what she needs, and have spoken to your SENDCo who has said that she will come and observe Mile.
>
> Recently, her foster mother has said to you that Mile does not seem to be able to hear very well and that this may be the cause of her language delay. She says that she will mention this to the GP.
>
> You are invited to come to a review meeting to discuss Mile's progress, as she has been in the setting for six months.
>
> Identify which other professionals might attend the meeting, and write a presentation which you will give them to outline her first six months and propose next steps.
>
> Discuss how this meeting will benefit Mile, her foster parents and the early years setting.

8 The importance of observations in early years childcare

Observing and assessing children is important for early years childcare. You will need to learn why observations are important, the different methods that can be used and how they are shared with others. You will also learn about the importance of accurate observations.

8.1 Observation and recording methods

REVISED

8.1.1 How observations support child development

An observation is what an adult notices about a child's behaviour, knowledge or development. Observations are used to help practitioners learn more about what children know and can do.

This information is used to assess children's progress. An assessment can then be used to work out the help, activities or resources which the child needs.

It is important to learn two terms for this unit:
+ Formative assessment – assessment that informs planning and immediate responses to children.
+ Summative assessment – assessment that provides a summary of the child's learning and development at a point in time.

> **Exam tip**
> Remember that both types of assessment are used by early years settings.

Formative assessment
Ongoing and in-the-moment assessment.

Summative assessment
An assessment which summarises the child's progress to date.

Formative assessment
This refers to assessment which informs planning and immediate responses to children. You need to learn six reasons why formative assessment is important.

Formative assessment is used to:
+ find out the child's interests – children learn more when they are interested
+ help identify stages of development – as this helps adults choose activities, resources and approaches
+ understand triggers in behaviour – sometimes by observing we can understand what makes a child show unwanted behaviour
+ gain insights to share with parents/carers/professionals – adults may observe something that parents and professionals will find helpful or interesting
+ support provision for the characteristics of effective teaching and learning
+ plan development activities – some children might need to do activities that will help them make progress in one or more area.

Characteristics of effective teaching and learning A term used in the EYFS to describe the skills and attitudes that children need to develop in order to learn, e.g. concentrating, persevering.

Summative assessment
A summative assessment provides a summary of a child's learning and development. An example of a summative assessment is a report at the end of a school term. You need to learn the five reasons why summative assessments are used by adults: see Figure 8.1.

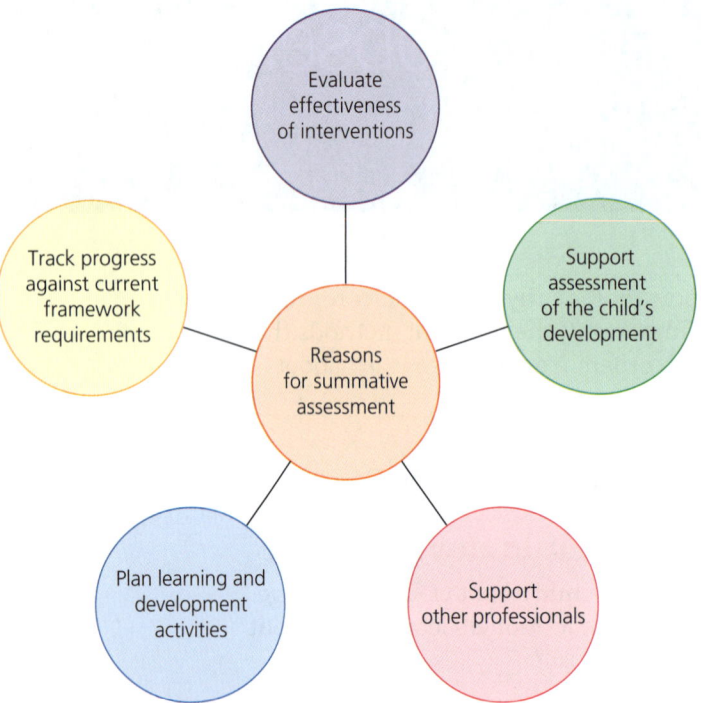

Figure 8.1 Reasons to carry out summative assessments

> ### Check your understanding
> 1. What is the difference between a formative and a summative assessment?

> ### Revision activity
> Copy out this table. In one column, from memory, write the six reasons why formative assessment is used. In the other column, again from memory, write the five reasons why summative assessment is used. Check the book to see how many you have remembered correctly.
>
> | Formative assessment is used to: | Summative assessment is used to |
> |---|---|
> | 1 | 1 |
> | 2 | 2 |
> | 3 | 3 |
> | 4 | 4 |
> | 5 | 5 |
> | 6 | |

> ### Check your understanding
> 2. Why might a physiotherapist need a summative assessment from a nursery of a child's communication and language?

8.1.2 Objective and subjective observation

All types of observation and assessment must be accurate. They cannot be subjective (based on opinions or feelings about e.g. a child). Inaccurate observations and assessments can mean that children do not get the help that they need. Objective observations are more accurate.

An objective observation:
+ is a record of what is seen and heard
+ does not include an opinion
+ states the facts and details only
+ avoids interpretation.

Subjective Based on opinions and feelings.

Objective Based on facts.

Check your understanding and progress at www.hoddereducation.co.uk/myrevisionnotes

Subjective observation means it is:
- influenced by past events
- based on personal experience
- based on opinion, feelings or assumption
- subject to interpretation.

> **Check your understanding**
>
> 3 A childminder has observed a three-year-old child. This is what has been written:
>
> *Darius plays with the Lego™ blocks. He turns over a box of bricks and puts the grey bricks to his left hand side. He puts bricks together and creates a complex model. He turns and says "I've made a spaceship."*
>
> Is this an example of an objective or subjective observation?

> **Revision activity**
>
> You will need eight cards. Copy out this list so that there is one statement on each card:
> - A record of what is seen and heard.
> - It does not include an opinion.
> - It states the facts and details only.
> - It avoids interpretation.
> - It is influenced by past events.
> - It is based on personal experience.
> - It is based on opinion, feelings or assumption.
> - It is subject to interpretation.
>
> Mix up the cards.
>
> Look at each and sort them into two piles: objective and subjective. When you have finished, check the book to see whether each card is in the right pile.

8.1.3 Components of recording observations

Observation is part of a process that also includes planning. There are four different steps or components, as listed below. (We look in more detail at the planning cycle and also how observations are assessed or evaluated in Chapter 9.)

- Aim – what needs to be observed.

  The adult has to decide what to watch out for. For instance, if a four-year-old child does not seem to play with other children, an adult may observe what the child does when other children play in the same space.

- Recording – the method used and the information gained.

  The adult has to decide which method to use and then carry out the observation.

- Evaluation – the assessment of what has been observed and recorded.

  The adult has to think about what they have found out about the child's development. This might include looking at the milestones (see page 14).

- Planning – consider what should happen next to support the child.

  The adult has to use their evaluation to work out what activities, support or resources the child needs next.

> **Typical mistake**
>
> Don't forget to include the role of evaluation and planning when talking about observations and assessments.

> **Check your understanding**
>
> 4 Write down the **four** components of an observation.

> **Revision activity**
>
> There is an order for the observation process. For example, you cannot record without first deciding on an aim. Look at these different components and write them down in the correct order:
>
> Evaluation   Planning   Recording   Aim

8.1.4 Different methods of observations

There are several different methods of recording observations. Early years settings often use more than one method to properly understand a child's development and interests.

You need to learn about five different methods.

Media methods

These could include films, photographs and written notes recorded on a tablet or PC.
- Media methods are usually quick and easy.
- They can be done with a tablet or phone.
- Some settings upload digital observations onto apps that track progress.
- They can be shared with parents and other professionals easily (see section 8.1.5).
- Confidentiality has to be maintained to protect images and information about the child and the family. Information must only be shared with parents and those professionals who have a right or permission to see it. (See Chapter 5.)

Learning journal

This consists of a collection of notes, observations and thoughts put into a book, app or digital document. It is often used to help formative assessment as it is ongoing.
- A journal provides a record of a child's time in a setting.
- This can encourage parents to take an interest in their child's development.
- It can be time-consuming as the journal needs to be kept up to date.

Sticky (e.g. Post-it®) notes

A note of a child's behaviour or something that they have done can be jotted down on a sticky note.
- This can be seen and shared with team members and parents.
- It is quick to create.
- It might not provide enough detail to be useful.
- Notes might be lost if not gathered in and filed quickly or correctly.

Narrative/free description/written account

Adults can write down what a child does and says for a short period or a set amount of time.
- This can provide a lot of information about a child's learning and development.
- It can help the adult to learn more about a child's interests and how they learn.
- It is hard to write down everything that the child does in the time.

Checklists
- These are used for ticking off or noting whether a child has developed a particular skill.
- They are designed to be easy to use.
- Using checklists can help adults to spot whether children are not showing expected progress.

Check your understanding and progress at www.hoddereducation.co.uk/myrevisionnotes

+ Checklists can be completed by adults asking children to do things, such as counting the number of cars that have been put out. If the child is not interested or becomes anxious, they might not complete the task. This means the results might not be accurate.

Three-year-old general checklist	Achieved?
Most of speech is clear enough for strangers to understand	☐
Says their own name and the names of their friends	☐
Can do a puzzle with 3–4 pieces	☐
Knows the difference between big and small	☐
Can retell the story in a book they were read	☐

Figure 8.2 A checklist is one way of recording information about a child's progress

Check your understanding

5 Match the observation method to the explanation.

Method		Explanation	
a	Checklist	1	Writing down what a child does and says for a short period or a set amount of time
b	Written account	2	A collection of notes, observations and thoughts put into a book or online program
c	Media method	3	Ticking off or noting whether a child has developed a particular skill
d	Sticky notes	4	Films, photographs and written notes recorded on a tablet or PC
e	Learning journal	5	A note of a child's behaviour or something that they have done, jotted down on a sticky note

6 Can you explain why a learning journal is an example of formative assessment?

Revision activity

Draw a spider diagram from memory that shows each of the five observation methods. You may want to illustrate the methods with small sketches to help you remember each one.

8.1.5 Sharing observations

Observations and assessments are shared with other adults. This includes team members, parents, health professionals and social workers.

You will need to learn why observations and assessments are shared with other adults. There are four key reasons, as shown in Table 8.1.

Continuity of care Making sure that adults take similar approaches to the needs of a child.

Table 8.1 Sharing observations and assessments

Reason for sharing	Explanation	Who they are shared with
Continuity of care	To make sure that everyone meets a child's needs in the same way. For example, following the same routines and approaches to managing behaviour.	+ Parents and carers + Adults in other settings that a child attends + Team members
Monitoring progress	Information can be brought together to track a child's development.	+ Parents and carers + Adults in other settings that a child attends + Team members + Health visitor
Early intervention	Sharing information with others can mean that a child who needs extra support receives it more quickly.	+ Parents and carers + Professionals including physiotherapists and educational psychologists + Adults in other settings that a child attends
Child-centred approach	This makes sure that children's needs and interests are met.	+ Parents and carers + Team members + Adults in other settings that a child attends

Revision activity

For each of these scenarios, give two reasons why a child will benefit if adults share observations:
- A child is not talking well for her age. She spends mornings at a pre-school and afternoons at a childminder.
- A baby is starting a nursery for the first time.

Check your understanding

7 Can you explain why sharing observations is important when children attend more than one setting?

Exam tip

When writing about sharing observations, remember to mention the importance of following confidentiality policies.

Exam-style questions

1 Explain the importance of objective observations. [2]
2 Give **two** features of a subjective observation. [2]
3 Identify **two** reasons why an early years setting might carry out formative assessments. [2]
4 Frankie is three years old. His key person and his parents are concerned about his behaviour at home and also at the nursery. He has been biting in the nursery and being aggressive towards his sister at home. They agree that the key person should carry out some observations of his behaviour.
   a) Identify **two** recording methods that might be used to observe Frankie's behaviour. [2]
   b) Discuss how these two recording methods might be used to support Frankie's development. [6]
5 Give **two** reasons why sharing accurate observations with parents and other professionals can benefit a child. [2]
6 Explain the difference between a checklist and a learning journal. [2]
7 Which of these describes an objective observation?
   A Influenced by past events
   B Includes judgements
   C Based on opinion and feelings
   D Is limited to what has been seen and heard [1]
8 A child goes to more than one early years setting. Evaluate the role of sharing observations with others. [6]
9 Give **one** example of a media method of observation. [1]
10 A four-year-old child is asked to count five objects. An adult notes whether the child can do this. Identify the observation method being used in this situation. [1]

Use your knowledge

Sara is three years old. She can walk, but often bumps into things. She climbs stairs slowly by holding onto an adult's hand. Sara's family live in a small flat in a high-rise building. Sara rarely plays outdoors because there is nowhere close by and the lift is often broken.

Sara has just started at a local nursery after seeing the health visitor. She has settled well at the nursery, although staff have noticed that she does not play with the other children.

The nursery has asked you to assist them in observing and assessing Sara's development as they are working closely with the health visitor.

You need to provide them with information that includes:
- the importance of assessing development
- expected milestones for physical, cognitive, communication and language, and social and emotional development for three-year-olds
- factors that might affect Sara's holistic development.

The nursery also want to create a plan for observing Sara. To help them, provide information about:
- the areas of Sara's development that might be a priority when writing aims for observations
- the methods that might be used to observe Sara
- the importance of remaining objective when observing
- how confidentiality and data protection procedures should be maintained when sharing information with the health visitor.

9 Planning in early years childcare

Planning is an important part of working with young children. Adults use the information from observations to help them plan and meet children's needs. You need to revise this chapter alongside Chapter 8.

9.1 The purpose of a child-centred approach

REVISED

The term 'child-centred' is often used in early years settings. It means that children's needs, wishes and interests are the priority for adults. It does not mean that children are able to do anything that they want!

Child-centred practice
Where an early years setting is using child-centred practice, everything is organised around the needs and interests of children. Here are some examples of child-centred practice:
+ Settling in is organised so that it goes at the pace of the child and their family.
+ Furniture and resources are organised so that children can be independent.
+ Adults listen to children and observe them so that they understand their feelings.
+ Routines are organised to meet individual children's needs; for example, a toddler might need a comforter at nap time.

> **Check your understanding**
>
> 1 A child only wants to eat biscuits. The child tells the adult that they don't like other food. The adult makes a smiley face using small amounts of fruit and vegetables. The child smiles and eats a grape from the plate.
>   a) Explain how the adult is using child-centred practice to meet the child's needs for health.
>   b) Why would it not be child-centred to give the child only biscuits?

> **Typical mistake**
>
> Don't think that a child-centred approach means that children are allowed to do anything. Children need to be kept safe and also healthy.

Child-centred approach to play
The term 'child-centred approach' is also used when planning for play. It means that children can choose what to play with and how they play.

The role of the adult is to:
+ support the child during their play
+ observe children's interests and their developmental needs.

A child-centred approach to play means that the environment has to be well planned. In order to choose toys and resources, children need to know what is there and be able to reach them.

> **Child-centred approach**
>
> Basing decisions around a child's needs, interests and opinions.

> **Revision activity**
>
> Write down 'Child-centred practice' on a sheet of paper. From memory, can you explain what this means for organising an early years setting?
>
> Now write down 'Child-centred approach to play'. From memory, explain what this means for children playing in a setting.

Figure 9.1 The adult is supporting these children as they play. This is an example of a child-centred approach

9.2 The purpose of the planning cycle

REVISED

Planning is a process. We look at this process in section 9.3. The process is known as the *planning cycle*. You will need to know why the planning cycle is important in early years settings and the different ways that it helps children.

Planning cycle The process that early years setting use to plan for children.

Six reasons for the planning cycle are given in the specification. You need to learn these: see Figure 9.2.

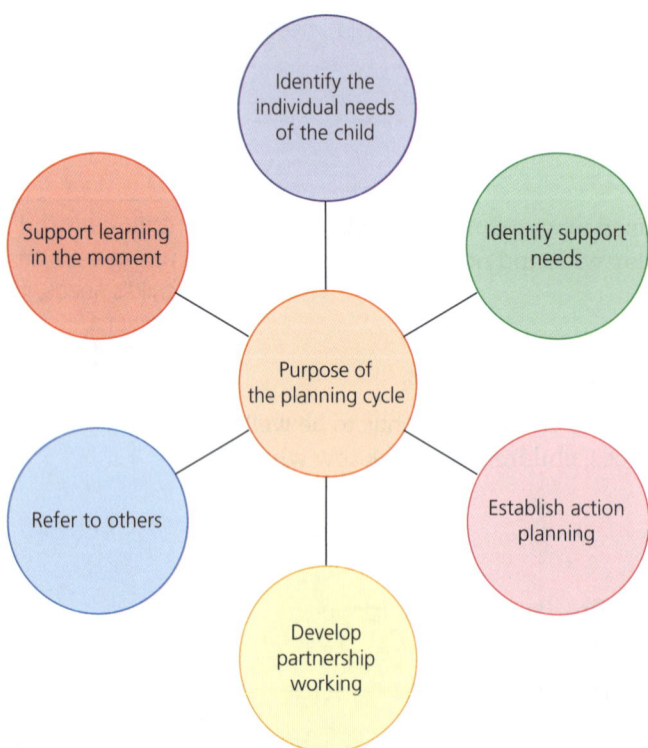

Figure 9.2 The purpose of the planning cycle

Identify the individual needs of the child

The planning cycle can be used to look at children's overall development as well as for individual areas of development. Table 9.1 shows some examples of how planning might identify a child's individual needs in overall development but also in each of the areas of development. You do not have to learn every example, but you might find that they help your understanding.

Table 9.1 How planning can support children's development

Area of development	Example
Holistic (overall) development	A child is new to the nursery. The key person observes what the child is interested in, how they use the equipment and resources and what skills they have. They use this information to create a plan.
Physical	A practitioner observes that a child wants to cut out using scissors, but has not yet developed the skills. The practitioner plans a simple activity involving scissors.
Cognitive	A child is fascinated by the ice on the outside of the window. The adult plans an activity involving ice so the children can learn more about its properties.
Communication and language	A three-year-old child has started with a childminder and is learning English. The childminder notices that the child likes playing with the trains. The childminder uses this information to develop the child's vocabulary by planning books and activities based on trains.
Social and emotional	A four-year-old child finds it difficult to play with other children because she is new to the nursery and has not had opportunities to be with other children. The practitioner observes situations when the child does play with another child. This information is used to set up more activities when the children can play together.

Identify support needs

The planning cycle is used to help children who have specific needs including SEND. The planning cycle can show how a child's progress can be monitored and how well the interventions are working.

Establish action planning

The planning cycle can be used for action planning. If a child has many different needs, adults might decide what to focus on. They can then review the child's progress and their responses.

> **Check your understanding**
>
> 2 A four-year-old child has communication and language delay. She also has some delay in her fine motor skills. The nursery has met her parents to work out how best to support her progress.
> Why is it important to use the planning cycle to create an action plan?

Develop partnership working

Other adults such as parents or other professionals might help with planning. Their observations about a child might be used when planning activities, resources and play opportunities. By involving other people, children's needs are more likely to be met as information is shared and also discussed.

Refer to others

The planning cycle is sometimes used when referring children to other professionals. For example, an educational psychologist might want to know what a nursery has already done to help a child.

> **Check your understanding**
>
> 3 In Chapter 7 we looked at specialist roles outside of the early years setting. What is the role of an educational psychologist?

Support learning in the moment

The specification for this qualification talks about **learning in the moment**. You need to learn what this term means as it is linked to a child-centred approach. You also need to know how the planning cycle is linked to learning in the moment.

The terms 'learning in the moment' and 'planning in the moment' are used in some (but not all) early years settings. The terms are used because adults are often responding to children's interests and needs as they play, to promote learning. Adults are able to do this because they closely observe and assess the child, and then use this information to work out how best to respond to the child. The adult might put out extra resources or answer a child's question to develop the child's learning.

> **Learning in the moment**
> Learning that happens as a result of child-centred interactions and a well-planned environment.

> **Check your understanding**
>
> 4 A child is playing with bricks. The child tells the adult that it is a house for a dinosaur. They talk about the size of house needed for a dinosaur. The adult gets out three different-sized dinosaurs. They explore which one will fit best in the house.
>   Why is this an example of learning in the moment?

To support learning in the moment, adults might also plan the environment in ways that will encourage the children to learn through play. This is known as a 'well-planned environment'. Adults might make changes to the environment as a result of observing and assessing children while the children are playing.

> **Revision activity**
>
> From memory, list the six reasons why the planning cycle is used in early years settings.
>
> Check what you have written. Focus your revision on those that you have missed.

9.3 The planning cycle

REVISED

There are five steps in the planning cycle. You will need to know about each step and its importance.

You will also need to learn how the planning cycle links to formative and summative assessment. You should have revised formative and summative assessment in Chapter 8.

> **Check your understanding**
>
> 5 What is meant by the term 'formative assessment'?

The planning cycle is often shown as a circle: see Figure 9.3. This is because the process is continuous. Make sure that you learn each of the steps and the order of the planning cycle.

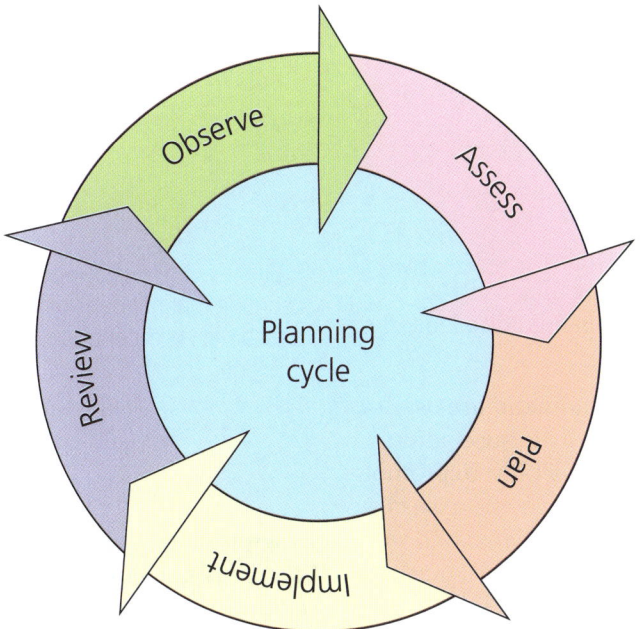

Figure 9.3 The planning cycle

Formative and summative assessment and the planning cycle

The planning cycle supports formative and summative assessment. You need to know how it supports both.

One of the most important steps of the planning cycle is for adults to observe children. This in turn means that the information that they learn can be used for both formative and summative assessment.

Remember: formative assessment is ongoing assessment, and summative assessment is a 'summing' up of the knowledge and skills.
+ By using the planning cycle, adults can make a formative assessment of children's ongoing progress.
+ They can also reflect on observations that have taken place in previous planning cycles to do a summative assessment.

Exam tip

Remember that parents and carers can also share their observations about their child at home as part of the planning cycle.

Check your understanding

6   A three-year-old is new to a pre-school. The key person is playing alongside him. He is observing how he communicates. Later in the day, he tries out a new activity with him. He notes how he responds and then uses this information to help him plan for his next session.

    Explain how the key person is using the planning cycle to support formative assessment.

Steps in the planning cycle

As well as learning the stages of the planning cycle, you will need to understand how it works in practice.

Observe

Adults observe children's development but also their interests and how they respond.

Revision activity

Write down two ways of recording an observation.

Look back at Chapter 8 to check your answer.

Figure 9.4 This activity has been planned to support children's social and physical development.

Assess

Adults have to think about what the observation of the child means. They need to think about how well the child is doing compared to:
+ expected key milestones of development
+ current framework expectations or requirements.

Where there are concerns, the adults then need to think about whether a child needs support or early intervention.

> **Revision activity**
>
> Write down what is meant by a framework expectation/requirement.
>
> Check your answer against the information in Chapter 8.

> **Check your understanding**
>
> 7 A practitioner has been working with a three-year-old, Lukasz. Lukasz is talking well, but is not able to run easily.
>   a) Using your knowledge about expected milestones from Chapter 1, identify whether Lukasz might need support or an early intervention.
>   b) Identify which areas of development need an early intervention.

Plan

This is the step when decisions are made about how best to support the child. Adults need to agree and record what the child needs. The spider diagram in Figure 9.5 shows what a plan may include.

> **Typical mistake**
>
> Don't write about planning without showing that it forms part of a cycle.

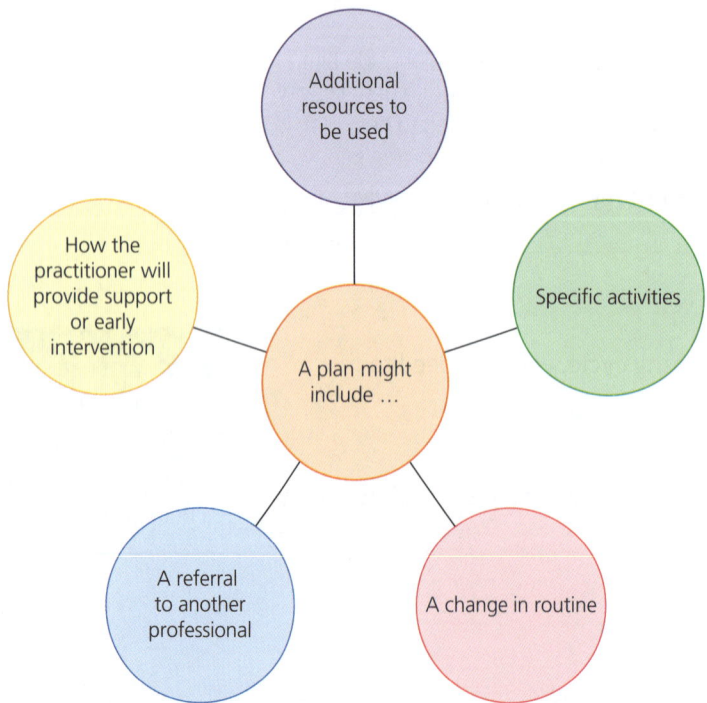

Figure 9.5 A typical plan to support a child

Check your understanding and progress at www.hoddereducation.co.uk/myrevisionnotes

> **Check your understanding**
>
> 8 A practitioner has observed that a two-year-old child often has a tantrum before lunchtime and also before teatime. What might be included in plan for this child?

> **Exam tip**
>
> When writing about the planning cycle, remember that plans might be complex. They might include specific activities and resources to be used as well as how the early years practitioner will provide support.

> **Revision activity**
>
>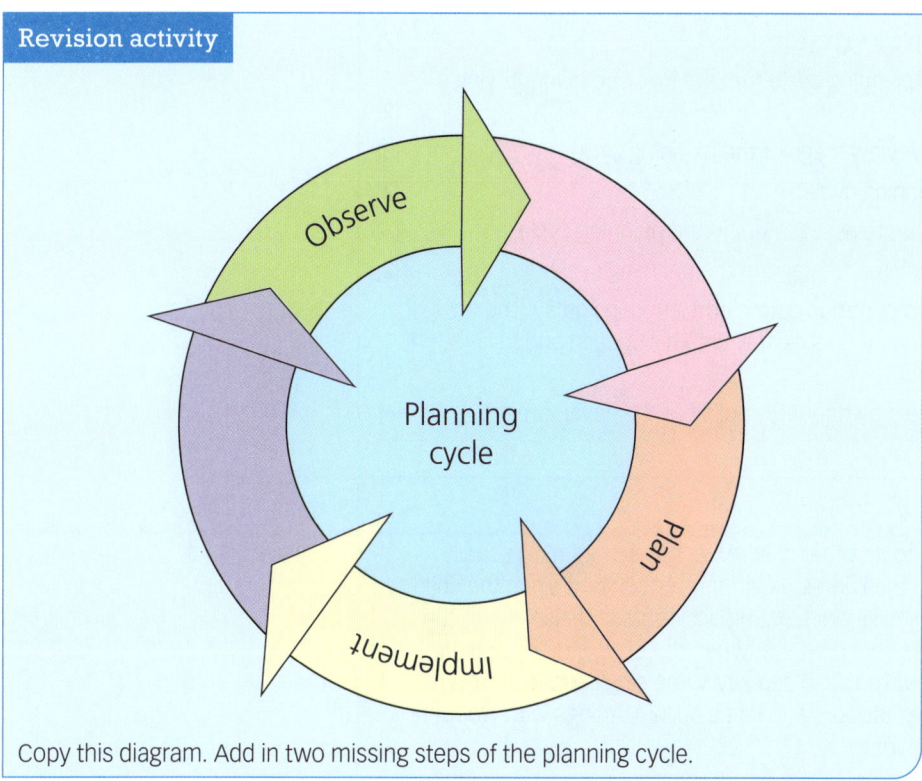
>
> Copy this diagram. Add in two missing steps of the planning cycle.

Implement

This is the 'action' step of the planning cycle. You need to remember three things about this step:
+ The plan needs to be put into practice.
+ It is shared with other professionals as well as parents/carers.
+ A record is kept of how the plan is put into action.

Review

This stage is about seeing how well the plan is working and what might need to be changed. You need to learn the four reasons for this:
+ Observe how well the child's needs have been met.
+ Make any adjustments to the plan.
+ Engage in partnership working (talking to parents, carers and other professionals about how the plan is working).
+ Opportunity for practitioner reflection (thinking about their role and what they have learnt).

> **Exam tip**
>
> In written answers about the planning cycle, remember that 'observe' always follows the 'review' stage.

> **Revision activity**
>
> + Create a diagram showing the planning cycle.
> + Next to each stage, write a short explanation. Check your work against this section.

Exam-style questions

1. Define the term 'child-centred approach'. [1]
2. Give **one** example of how a setting may show child-centred practice. [1]
3. Discuss how the planning cycle supports learning in the moment. [6]
4. Outline the **five** stages of the planning cycle. [2]
5. Identify the **two** stages of the planning cycle that are involved in identifying a child's stage of development. [2]
6. Explain the importance of the review stage of the planning cycle. [3]
7. State **two** purposes of the planning cycle. [2]
8. Discuss the importance of accurate assessment in the planning cycle. [6]
9. Explain the purpose of the 'implement' stage of the planning cycle. [2]
10. Amol is four years old. He has a communication and language delay. The nursery uses a planning cycle and works closely with his speech and language therapist and his parents.
    Discuss how the planning cycle may benefit Amol's holistic development. [6]

Use your knowledge

A three-year-old child has started to hit other children at pre-school. This usually happens indoors and often before mealtimes. Their parents say that since the child's baby sister was born, the child has frequent toileting accidents and also is attention-seeking. The child's key person has observed that when the child is doing activities in small groups their behaviour is fine. The child can say some single words, but is not using sentences. They enjoy being outdoors and loves building things with wooden blocks. The child finds it hard to share toys.

The pre-school has asked you for some advice.

Write a report with information about:
+ the child's stage of development compared to expected milestones
+ factors that might affect this child's stage of development
+ how observations may be used to inform the planning cycle, with suggestions of methods
+ ways in which the planning cycle may be used to support this child
+ any other issues that the pre-school may need to consider, such as safeguarding.

Check your understanding and progress at www.hoddereducation.co.uk/myrevisionnotes

Glossary

Accident An unintended incident which may cause physical injury.

Active listening Giving people your full attention and listening to them carefully.

Adult–child ratio How many staff there are to children. For example, a ratio of 1:3 would mean that there is one adult member of staff to every three children.

Anti-discriminatory Ways of working with children and their families that are inclusive and promote equality and diversity.

Asymmetric tonic neck reflex (ATNR) A reflex where if the baby's head is turned to one side, the knee and arm on the other side bend.

Attention deficit hyperactivity disorder (ADHD) A condition that means that children find it hard to sit and concentrate and therefore need to learn in different ways.

Bereavement The death of a person or pet.

Biological influences Things that are a result of the way that we have been made.

Breach Failure to keep to an agreement.

Characteristics of effective teaching and learning A term used in the EYFS to describe the skills and attitudes that children need to develop in order to learn, e.g. concentrating, persevering.

Child-centred Putting the needs of the child first and encouraging them to be independent.

Child-centred approach Basing decisions around a child's needs, interests and opinions.

Child-centred practice Decisions are based on the needs and interests of the child

Chronic illness A health problem that is either long-term or comes back repeatedly.

Confidentiality The preservation of privileged information concerning children and their families.

Continuity of care Making sure that adults take similar approaches to the needs of a child.

Cruise How babies walk about by holding onto furniture.

Designated safeguarding lead (DSL) The person in the setting who is responsible for acting on and monitoring any safeguarding concerns.

Discriminate To treat someone differently based on a characteristic such as race, gender or disability.

Diversity The range of values, attitudes, cultures and beliefs held by different people.

Eczema A skin condition that causes dry and itchy skin.

EHCP (Education, Health and Care Plan) A document which outlines the care and support a child or young person will need in order to meet their potential up to the age of 25.

Embellishment A decoration which has been added to something.

Emotional wellbeing A state of good mental health.

Enabling environment An environment that supports children's learning and independence.

English as an additional language (EAL) When someone speaks English but it is not their first language.

Environmental influences Things that have happened and are happening to a child that will affect their development.

Equality Individuals are treated in the same way.

External professional A professional working with children and families who is not based in a setting.

Family dynamic The way relationships work in a family.

Fine motor skills Co-ordination of small muscles, precise movements and hand–eye co-ordination.

Formative assessment Ongoing and in-the-moment assessment.

Framework A set of standards that must be met.

Genes Chromosomes that contain instructions about whether and how cells grow.

Genetic Relating to genes.

Gross motor skills Co-ordination of the large muscles of the arms, legs and torso.

Holistic development How different aspects of development are linked together.

Incident An event which may cause an injury or develop into an emergency.

Inclusive Open to and including everyone.

Inherited characteristics Things that can be traced back to a child's biological family.

Inhibited relationships When a child cannot trust others and therefore is not as close to others as they could be.

Intervention In an education context, an intervention is usually a short series of activities designed to support a child's needs.

Language-rich environment An environment with a lot of talking and interaction between children and other people.

Glossary

Learning in the moment Learning that happens as a result of child-centred interactions and a well-planned environment.

Legislation A law or set of laws that have been passed by Parliament.

Lines of reporting The order or direction in which information is passed on.

Malpractice A failure to carry out professional duties and acting in a way which causes harm.

Media Different ways in which creativity is expressed, for example painting, drawing or music.

Milestones Skills that are expected at different ages.

Moro reflex A reflex where the baby throws back head and arms, then brings them in before crying.

Notifiable disease A disease which must be reported by law to the authorities. A full list can be found at www.gov.uk/guidance/notifiable-diseases-and-causative-organisms-how-to-report#list-of-notifiable-diseases

Objective Based on facts.

Ofsted Office for Standards in Education, Children's Services and Skills. This is a regulatory authority.

Open door policy People are always welcome to talk to the setting about any questions or concerns whenever they have them, without waiting to be invited to comment.

Open-ended talk Questions and conversations which do not have a 'yes' or 'no' answer.

Palmar grasp Object is held in the child's fist.

Personal qualities An individual's characteristics and personality traits.

Physiological Related to the body, and the way in which living things work or what they need to survive (for example air, water, food, sleep, exercise and shelter).

Pincer grip Object is held between thumb and forefinger or middle finger.

Planning cycle The process that early years settings use to plan for children.

Policy An agreed set of actions that have been adopted by an organisation to deal with certain situations.

Poverty Living on a very low income and/or not having what you need.

Primitive reflexes Movements that newborns make automatically.

Private Profit-making business where services are chargeable.

Procedure The way in which an organisation carries out a policy.

Professional Behaving in a way which shows you are competent and reliable in your job role.

Psychological Relating to or affecting the mind.

Ratified Formally agreed by government.

Reasonable adjustments Removing barriers and putting measures in place so that an individual can take part in an activity.

Reduced educational attainment Children not doing as well at school as they are able.

Regression Aspects of a child's development going backwards.

Regulatory authority A group which monitors standards in particular professions or organisations, such as health or education.

Resilience Being able to cope with setbacks.

Responsible person Someone in the setting who has a particular responsibility, for example health and safety or first aid.

Risk assessment A process to identify existing or potential hazards, and to consider the risk of harm.

Rooting A reflex in newborn babies to search for milk using their mouth.

Rural In the countryside.

Safeguarding The term to use when talking about keeping children safe from abuse or neglect, and protecting them from harm.

Scaffold Provide support for learning by breaking it into smaller steps.

SEND Special educational needs and disabilities.

Sensory play A type of play which encourages children to learn using their senses. Some examples include using dough or water, or making shakers.

Statutory Required by law and funded by the government.

Subjective Based on opinions and feelings.

Summative assessment An assessment which summarises the child's progress to date.

Transition The change from one stage or state to another.

Voluntary Charities and not-for-profit organisations set up to meet the needs of children and their families.

Vulnerability Higher chance of something negative happening.

Whistleblowing Reporting malpractice or wrongdoing of someone in your own workplace.

Index

abuse 25, 63, 70–1
accessibility, early years provision 56
accidents 62, 67
achievement 41
active listening 79
adapting activities 63–4, 68–9, 86
affection 41
age, starting school 55
alcohol 25
anti-discriminatory practice 69
appearance, of practitioner 75
assessments
    formative 93, 103
    summative 93–4, 103
    see also observations; planning cycle
asymmetric tonic neck reflex 16
attachment 28–30, 37
Attention deficit hyperactivity
    disorder (ADHD) 28
babies, primitive reflexes 16
balance 44
basic care needs 40
    see also care routines
behaviour management 48
belonging 41
bereavement 32, 37
biological influences 21–3, 27–9
body art 75
body language 80
boundaries 41, 77
care needs 40
care routines 42–3, 67, 86
checklists 96–7
child-centred approach 36, 45, 88, 97, 99–100
child development
    biological influences 21–3, 27–9
    cognitive 12, 16–17, 34, 52, 101
    communication and language 12, 17–18, 34, 45, 52, 101
    environmental influences 21–7, 29–31
    holistic 12–13, 52, 101
    impact of transitions 33–5
    milestones 14–18, 29–31
    nature and nurture 21–7
    physical 12, 14–15, 33, 52, 101
    social and emotional 12, 18, 29, 34–5, 52, 101
    socio-economic factors 24–7
childminders 53, 55, 84
cognitive development 12, 16–17, 34, 52, 101
communication and language
    development 12, 17–18, 34, 45, 52, 101
communication, practitioner role 78–80
concentration 28, 34, 46
confidence 41, 44–5

confidentiality 65, 71–3, 77
consent 65
continuity of care 97
co-operation 48
co-ordination 44, 46
creative play 45
crèche 55
Data Protection Act 2018 65, 72
DBS (Disclosure and Barring Service) 65
designated safeguarding lead (DSL) 63, 85, 90
development see child development
diet 25, 29, 67
    see also food and drink
dignity 69, 77
disclosures 65
discrimination 63, 64, 69
diversity 63–4, 69
drugs 25
Duchenne muscular dystrophy 23
Early Years Foundation Stage (EYFS) 53–4, 65
early years practitioner 83–4
    see also practitioner role
early years provision
    accessibility 55–6
    admissions criteria 56
    choosing 55–8
    purpose of 52–3
    settings 55
    types of 51
eczema 22, 28
educational attainment 28
EHCP (Education, Health and Care Plan) 91
emotional abuse 70
emotional development see social and emotional development
emotional safety 41
emotional wellbeing 31, 35
    see also wellbeing
enabling environments 86
English as an additional language (EAL) 69
environmental influences 21–7, 29–31
environments
    early years provision 56–7
    safety of 47–8
equality 63–4, 68
Equality Act 2010 63–4
equipment 52, 67
exercise 26, 41, 86
eye colour 23
family
    change of circumstance 37
    and development 25
    partnership working 88–9
family support worker 92

fine motor skills 14, 44, 46
first aid 67
food and drink 61–2, 67, 85
    see also diet
formative assessment 93, 103
general practitioner (GP) 91
genes 21
gross motor skills 14–15
hair colour 23
health 29–31, 44, 85
    see also wellbeing
health and safety
    accidents 62, 67
    legislation 61–2
    procedure 66–7
    risk assessments 47, 62, 66
    see also policies and procedures
Health and Safety at Work etc. Act 1974 61–2
health visitor 91
holistic development 12–13, 52, 101
hospital admission 37
hygiene
    personal 75
    routines 67, 86
illness 29, 33
imaginative play 46
inclusion 48, 64, 69
independence 48
individual needs 101
information, security of 65
inherited characteristics 21–3
inhibited relationships 28
interventions 88
job roles 83–4, 90–2
key person 65, 84, 90
language development see communication and language development
language-rich environment 26
learning difficulties 28
learning in the moment 102
learning journal 96
legislation 60–5
lifestyle 25
listening 79–80
manager 83
Maslow's Hierarchy of Needs 40–1
mental illness 29
milestones 14–18, 29–31
mobile phones 65–6, 77
Montessori 53
Moro reflex 16
motor skills 14–15, 44, 46
nanny 84
neglect 25, 70
new baby 37
notifiable diseases 67
nursery 55
observations

Index

methods 96–7
recording 95
sharing 97
see also assessments; planning cycle
off-site procedures 67
Ofsted (Office for Standards in Education, Children's Services and Skills) 60
open-ended conversations 48
paediatrician 91
palmar grasp 14
parents
  partnership working 88–9
  support for 53
partnership working 87–90, 101
personal hygiene 75
personal protective equipment (PPE) 67
physical abuse 70
physical activity and nutrition co-ordinator (PANCo) 90
physical development 12, 14–15, 33, 52, 101
physical play 44
physical safety 41
physiological needs 40
piercings 75
pincer grip 14
planning cycle 100–5
play 26, 44
  creative 45
  imaginative 46
  physical 44
  right to 63
  role of practitioner 47–9
  sensory 44, 46
policies and procedures 60–5, 67–8
poverty 24
practitioner role
  appearance 75–6
  attendance and punctuality 80–1
  behaviour 76

communication 78–80, 86
health and safety 67, 85
job roles 83–4
personal qualities 77–8
play activities 47–9, 86
positive attitude 77–8
promoting development 52, 86
responsibilities 85–7
as role model 35, 64
pre-school 55
primary school 55
primitive reflexes 16
problem solving 45, 48
professional boundaries 77
protected characteristics 64
provision *see* early years provision
psychological needs 40, 41
punctuality 81
reasonable adjustments 68
see also adapting activities
referrals 101
regression 33
regulatory authority 60
relationships
  importance of 26–7
  inhibited 28
  and play 46
  professional boundaries 77
Reporting of Injuries, Diseases and Dangerous Occurrences Regulations (RIDDOR) 2013 62, 67
resilience 35
respect 69, 77, 80
responsible person 66
rest 41
rights of children 62–3
risk assessments 47, 62, 66
role models 35, 64
room leader 84
rooting 16
routines *see* care routines

safeguarding 63, 65–6, 70–3, 88
  abuse 25, 63, 70–1
  disclosures 65
  whistleblowing 73
scaffolding 48
security
  of information 65
  of setting 67
  see also visitors
self-esteem 41
SEND (special educational needs and disabilities) 80
sensory play 44, 46
separation 37
settings 55
sexual abuse 70
sleep 41
social and emotional development 12, 18, 29, 34–5, 52, 101
social media 77
social worker 91
special educational needs and disabilities co-ordinator (SENDCo) 90
speech *see* communication and language development
staff–child ratio 65, 80
starting new childcare setting 37
stimulation 26
summative assessment 93–4, 103
tattoos 75
teaching assistant 84
timekeeping 81
transitions 31–7, 86
United Nations Convention on the Rights of the Child (UNCRC) 1989 62–3
visitors 61–2, 67
waste disposal 67
weight 29, 31
wellbeing 29, 31, 35, 44, 85
whistleblowing 73

Photo credits

p.13 © Jacob Crees-Cockayne/Hodder Education; **p.19** © DragonImages/stock.adobe.com; **p.22** © gamelover/stock.adobe.com; **p.45** © Africa Studio/stock.adobe.com; **p.52** © Jacob Crees-Cockayne/Hodder Education; **p.57** © Jules Selmes/Hodder Education; **p.62** © Oksana Kuzmina/stock.adobe.com; **p.68** © H. Mark Weidman Photography / Alamy Stock Photo; **p.76** © Jules Selmes/Hodder Education; **p.78** © Diego Cervo/stock.adobe.com; **p.79** © Jules Selmes/Hodder Education; **p.85** © Jacob Crees-Cockayne/Hodder Education; **p.87** © Jules Selmes/Hodder Education; **p.89** © Picture Partners/Alamy Stock Photo; **p.91** © Jules Selmes 2014/Hodder Education; **p.100** © Jacob Crees-Cockayne/Hodder Education; **p.104** © Visions of America, LLC / Alamy Stock Photo

Notes